The Interest Direct:

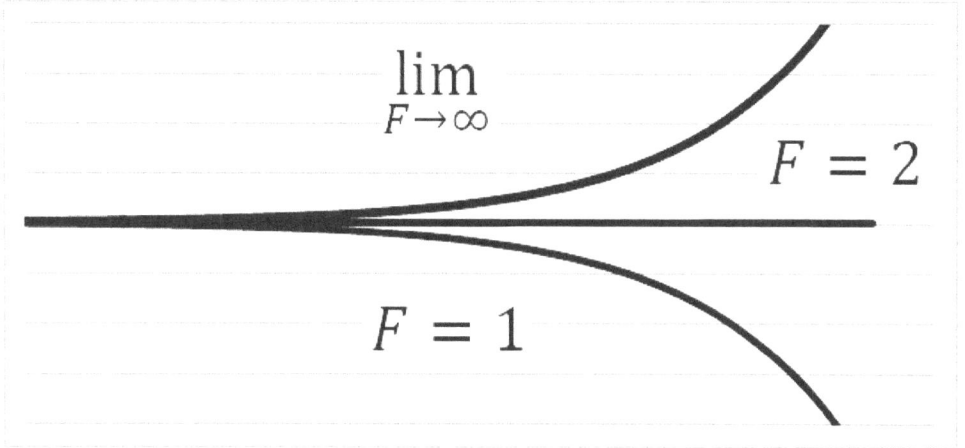

An Intuitively Obvious Approach to a Basic Understanding of the Interest for the Casual Observer

By John Weiss
2012

Preface:

The financial crisis of 2008 is, like every event in history, a great tool for learning. I personally learned two very important things. First – there are greedy people who try to take as much money as they can from anyone regardless of the long term consequences. Second – there are ignorant people who accept contractual debt obligations that almost guarantees unsustainable indentured servitude. Greed and ignorance caused the financial crisis, pure and simple.

Greed is an external calamity since it seeks to take away from others. We cannot rid ourselves of an external problem like greed because the fault does not lie within our sphere of influence. Human nature has been greedy for eons and the likes of Gandhi, Buddha, Confucius, and even Jesus Christ himself haven't been able to change it. As such I don't even pretend to be able to fix greed.

Ignorance, on the other hand, is an internal failing because ignorance squanders what is yours. I suspect a great deal of lendees agreed to such ruinous terms because they didn't understand the fundamental mathematics associated with interest bearing debt. But there is hope! Ignorance contains the wonderful characteristic of residing within your sphere of influence. If one could comprehend the basic mathematics of interest bearing loans then a person could understand the long term ramifications and competently balance the rewards and risks associated with it. Ideally they would even regulate the lending business by only accepting sound financial policy for the good of themselves and, indirectly, the financial system as a whole. It is to this end that this book is fashioned.

This book intends to provide a basic mathematical understanding of the underlying rules of interest bearing accounts taking no prior understanding of mathematics for granted. This book is written for the common 'dyscalculia' notoriously weak in mathematics. It is also written for the non-traditional but curious layman without time or resources to attend a formal instructional setting to explore the mathematics of interest. It is hoped that once the reader conquers this basic treatise on interest then they will have the necessary skills to explore connected topics in finance. As such, this book is not meant as an end all text, but as a beginning.

However, this book is NOT a magical bullet. You will still need to study the material in earnest to learn it. I have not come across a way for instant understanding of the mathematics of interest without work and perseverance. Although few chapters may seem difficult to you at first, I assure you that all topics are well within your ability.

This book is also NOT meant to show you how to become rich or advise you on which decisions are best for your specific situation so that you can be rich. Nor is this book written to pull you out of debt, or erase your debt, or even which decisions are best for your specific situation so that you can get out of debt. I have also tried to stay neutral on the politics of interest throughout this text. My main goal is to simply explain the process and theory of interest and not to dictate on the morality or legality of the matter. I will say that most major religions specifically ban usury, but I will also say that credit has facilitated social mobility in more than one case.

This book is only intended to explain the fundamental guidelines of the mathematical system of money and the interest it incurs. Although this book admittedly lacks the sex appeal of 'get rich quick' texts, I feel the information held within is much more valuable in the long run. Besides, all get rich quick texts are really only written to get one person rich; the author.

Best of luck,
John Weiss

Chapter 1: Addition

Before we begin in earnest, I should repeat a very important point mentioned in the preface. Due to the length of the equations contained in this book, it may be better to view the kindle version of this book in the landscape setting.

Don't worry if you didn't see it, I never read the preface either.

Section 1.1 – Defining a number:

How much do I owe?

How much do I have?

These two simple questions dictate a large portion of our lives. Both are a question about how large a value a thing contains. But to produce an accurate measurement of worth, it is necessary to first define what we will use to measure with. Modern society has decided on the fiat money supply, but it hasn't always been this way. Societies of the past have used gold, silver, copper, grain, cows, and even salt as a currency. For this text, we will use the simple square as a hypothetical currency that we can use to visually represent the fundamental mathematical operations. But first we will need to define what a number is.

The act of 'defining a number' may seem like a worthless endeavor, but the results of this section will be used as the foundation for the second section, which will serve as the foundation for the third, then the fourth and so on and so on. In fact the understanding of advanced mathematics is usually predicated upon a person's comprehension of the formative levels. Thus time invested in the beginning will pay dividends in later sections. I do not mean to be patronizing, only to argue why study should be applied to these 'worthless' sections.

Section 1.2 The number system:

It has been said that in the beginning there was nothing. As this was a fine place to begin the universe, so too shall it be a fine place to start the number system. We call this antithesis of being zero. Thus we can mathematically describe the state of having no money as:

$$worth = 0$$

We call this particular statement an equation because it utilizes an equal sign for its relationship. The equal sign (=) denotes a convergence of the two ideas that flank it, in this case the word 'worth' and the symbol '0'. Conceptually this means that at our current state we have no currency. The equal sign is a powerful symbol in mathematics because it specifies exact congruence – that the two flanking ideas are one in the same. So strong is this property that once two ideas are shown to be equal then they may be interchanged at will.

Let's use the equals sign to state something trivially obvious; a thing is equal to itself. To do this we would write

Equation 1.1

$$x = x$$

This may not be very ground breaking stuff to you and I, but some mathematicians actually require this as a property. It is called the reflexive property of equality, a part of the equivalence properties of equality. But before we bash our mathematicians too hard for being overly zealous it would be important to note that mathematics does not derive truth from 'obvious' standards. It is a quest to understand quantitative logic objectively and outside of your experience. For instance, could you draw a triangle with three right angles? Could you construct a one sided object? A person living in reality would say no to both of these questions based upon 'obvious' facts and experience. Luckily the mathematician does not live in reality. They saw that these questions could be answered with the spherical trigonometry and the Mobius strip respectively. This ability to suspend 'obvious' and natural gut reaction is necessary to fully grasp the mathematics of interest calculations. Instead, we must rely on compelling mathematical arguments. In a sense we will let the math lead us rather than force it where it will not go. More on this idea later.

To get back to the point, let us introduce a single unit of currency into the void that we call zero. Doing this will produce:

Figure 1.1 – One Unit of Worth

We call this single square 1 unit of currency, which corresponds with an increase in the value we possess. Since we hold this currency as our own, we will call this currency 'wealth'. Thus mathematically our worth is equal to one unit of wealth.

$$worth = 1$$

Notice that we stated we had an *increase* in value. An increase would infer that a larger amount is present than was held before. This brings up another type of relationship symbol; the inequality. The inequality functions in much the same way as an equal sign, but does not denote a convergence. Instead the inequality specifies which number, or in later chapters which condition, is larger in respect to another. By our understanding, the state of owning 1 unit of currency contains more value than 0 units of currency. Because of this, we could use the inequality sign to express the relationship between 0 and 1. We do this like so:

$$1 > 0$$

This inequality symbol is known as 'greater than' and specifies that the left hand side, 1, is of a larger value than the right hand side, 0. We could also have utilized the 'less than' sign like so:

$$0 < 1$$

This means that zero is less than one, which is also true. Either way we have successfully presented that the worth of the number 1 is greater than zero.

We now wish to introduce another identical square of currency into our argument to bring our total amount of squares to 2. Doing this will create a stack of currency like so:

Figure 1.2 – Two Units of Worth

And notice that the height of the currency has now increased to two units of currency stacked together:

$$worth = 2$$

What's more, we know that 2 is worth more than 1 because we increased a unit of currency to what was defined as 1 and so we can write:

$$2 > 1$$

Or equally true:

$$1 < 2$$

Let's repeat this process and introduce another identical square into the chain.

Figure 1.3 – Three Units of Worth

The amount of currency present is now 3, as can easily be verified by counting the number of squares. Notice also that the number 3 has a stack of currency that reaches higher than the number 2. Again, since we have increased the amount of currency available we can say that 3 is larger than 2.

$$3 > 2$$

Often times in mathematics an in depth understanding of a particular concept is directly under our nose. One such concept has been steadily gaining traction through our argument. To define this concept we must recall that two things happen each time we introduce another square of currency. First, and most obvious, is that the height of the stack increases. Second is that the resulting number is greater, or worth more, than the previous number. 3 was greater than 2, which is greater than 1, which is greater than 0. Thus we have created a way to define the 'greatness' of any number by measuring the height of a stack relative to other stacks of currency. This means that a number is only 'greater than' another number if the stack of currency associated with it is higher. This may not seem like much, but it will help tremendously later on.

Another property of numbers that has been simmering under our nose is actually the main goal of our argument; an objective definition of a number. Recall that the number 1 symbolized a single unit of currency. The number 2 represented a stack of currency two units high while the number 3 had a stack of currency containing three units. Taking this line of thought for granted, we can define a number like five as:

Figure 5.1 – Five Units of Worth

$$worth = 5$$

In this way the symbol '5' is only a representation of five units of currency stacked atop each other. But we needn't stop with five, we could easily say that 7 represents seven units of currency stacked together, 1000 is the symbol for one thousand units of currency stacked together, 900000 is the symbol for nine hundred thousand units of currency, etc, etc, etc. Thus we could conceivably define any numerical symbol by a particular height of currency and any integer, a whole number without a decimal, with a particular string of unit currencies. This then provides us with our desired definition of a number for this text: A number is simply a symbolic representation for a particular height of a stack of currency.

It would be nice if we only dealt with readily countable numbers because we could easily draw a small amount of squares stacked atop each other. But this text will often deal with numbers that are too large to show pictorially. For instance, 900000 is easy enough to write as a symbol, but only a fool would attempt to draw each and every square. Instead, this text will utilize the ellipses in place of what would otherwise be a great multitude of units of currency. This will allow us to represent such large numbers as, say 1000, easily and with little confusion.

Figure 1.5 – 1000 Units of Worth

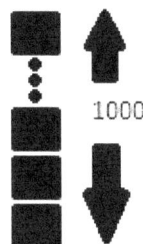

$$worth = 1000$$

The ellipses have been adopted by the technical community to instruct the reader to continue the 'obvious' pattern. In this case the ellipses mean that each and every needed square is accounted for within the stack of currency but we have decided not to show them. We instead only give an appreciable amount of information and use the ellipses to let the reader fill in the rest. Obviously the height of the stack of currency no longer truly reflects the worth of the number, but that is no matter. The key is that the information is understandable. But if the actual height doesn't necessarily change the understanding of the number, then couldn't we use the same picture to represent a completely different number? Couldn't we write something like:

Figure 1.6 – 1000000 units of worth

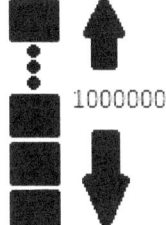

$$worth = 1000000$$

The above picture represents one million units of currency. In actual terms, the height of one million units of currency completely dwarfs a stack of ten thousand units. Yet we were still able to represent both values by the same picture. But why stop at a million? We could easily have used the same picture above and labeled the chain as ten million, or even a billion without loss of the idea. In fact, let's simply assume that the ellipses go on forever, or that the picture represents a stack of currency that never ends.

Figure 1.7 – An Infinite Amount of Wealth

$$worth = infinity = \infty$$

We call this obscenely large number infinity and it is symbolized by the sideways eight at the far right of the equation. It is considered the largest number, much bigger than any number we could ever encounter. Obviously stacking an infinite amount of currency is not physically possible, nor could we even write such a large number numerically. But with a distinctly human ability we can allow for the thought of such an occurrence and even manipulate equations in such a way to take into account an infinite phenomenon. But we won't explore such things… yet.

We could even go one step further. Let's use the ellipses to help construct a variable quantity. A variable is an unknown, but concrete, quantity that populates the formulas of interest mathematics. That's not to say that it's impossible to find out the value of a variable, as much of mathematics is specifically concerned with this conundrum, but only that we don't know the exact value at this particular point in time. To construct the variable quantity we simply use a chain of currency with ellipses to denote that we continue the obvious pattern for some unknown distance.

Figure 1.8 – A Variable Amount

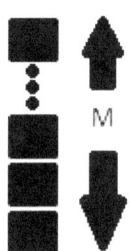

$$worth = M$$

Here we have defined the variable amount to be M, but it needn't be the only choice. Any letter in any alphabet, whether it is Greek, Latin, Japanese, or whatever other symbol you'd like to use, can represent a variable quantity. However, it is necessary to maintain continuity once we specify a variable to represent some idea in an argument. That is to say, the same variable represents exactly the same thing if written in two different parts of a formula. Once a new argument is started then the variables are again wiped clean and may be assigned at will to new ideas. One should be aware however that there are some variables that have come to define certain ideas and may promote confusion if used wantonly. For instance the symbol π has been adopted to represent the ratio of the diameter of a circle to its circumference, approximated to be 3.14. The variable e has been used extensively to symbolize Euler's constant, approximated to 2.718.

Thus we have developed a way to measure the worth of a number by the length of a chain of currency squares stacked atop each other. Larger chains of squares correlate to larger numerical worth and smaller chains of squares represent small numbers. This answers one of the two questions that began this chapter. How much do I have?

We now turn our attention to the former question; how much do I owe?

Section 1.3 - Negative numbers:

Let us define currency we owe as debt. For sake of continuity we will define the measurement of debt in a similar manner that we measured wealth above. Yet for obvious reasons, debt is intrinsically different from wealth. Thus we will opt for an unshaded square to differentiate debt from the shaded square used for wealth. This new representation will allow us to mirror our argument above and yet still allow for new and exciting possibilities.

Let us assume that we begin with owing nothing. Keeping with our prior assumption that nothing is defined to be zero we can list our current worth as:

$$worth = 0$$

Let us imagine that we introduce 1 unit of debt into our argument. Pictorially we would have:

Figure 1.9 – One Unit of Debt

Now, just as we had to tweak the pictorial representation of debt currency, we will need to also massage the mathematical number to reflect the new reality. We accomplish this by placing a simple dash before the number.

$$worth = -1$$

We call this number negative one and it represents one unit of debt. We have so far discussed two numbers that are associated with debt, 0 and (-1). But which of these numbers contains more value? Obviously owing nothing is much better than owing something. Thus we can assume without much difficulty that 0 has a greater value than negative one. Mathematically we would write this as:

$$0 > -1$$

Notice that with debt, a higher structure corresponds with less worth. This is in direct contrast with the wealth currency where height meant value. Keep this in mind as we progress through our argument. Following the same process as before, we will introduce another unit of debt currency to the first unit.

Figure 1.10 – Two Units of Debt

$$worth = -2$$

And we now have 2 units of debt, or a worth of negative 2. Since the structure is higher than the negative one structure, and because we are dealing with debt, we will define negative two to be less than negative one in value

$$-2 < -1$$

Or equivalently:

$$-1 > -2$$

We could continue this process of introducing more and more units of debt and we would move higher and higher until we hit negative infinity, the largest amount of debt possible and therefore the least number. Doing this would produce a second number tower that contains all of the negative numbers.

Figure 1.11 – Infinite Debt Tower

$$worth = -\infty$$

So now we have two towers that can help us measure the money we own and the money we owe. But looking closely at the two towers we notice that both towers begin with the number zero. This can serve a common base point and prompts the following figure.

Figure 1.12 – The Two Towers

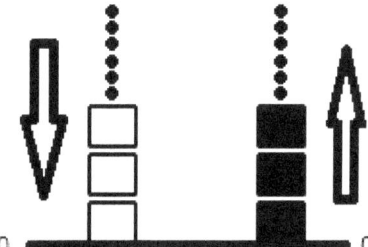

As shown, zero is a very special number. It is the symmetry point for the value of numbers. Everything greater than zero is a positive number and is concerned with wealth, while everything less than zero is negative and is associated with debt. The two arrows next to the towers show the direction of increasing value. This structure is a very important tool for mathematics as it easily and convincingly places every whole number, or integer, in order of greater value to lesser value depending upon where the integer is in relation to another. Notice that the least number, negative infinity, is high up in the top left corner. The value of the integers increase as we progress downwards towards zero, then circle back up the wealth tower towards positive infinity in the top right corner. The sequence would create a U shape if you traced it with your finger. Using our two towers we can easily say that -26 is much less than 2 for the simple fact that 2 is further along the U shape of the two towers. In fact we could easily point out that any positive number is greater than any negative number based upon this premise. Intuitively this should make sense. Would you rather have a dollar to your name or owe someone else a million dollars? For me the choice is clear.

Section 1.4 – Addition

We have now successfully derived a way to measure the worth of a given amount of currency by placing it within a number tower. But unfortunately for us, the two number towers are an arithmetic tool and does not allow us to progress into the general mathematics of interest. The reason we cannot progress further into mathematics is because a number is concrete in nature. 1 is 1 and 2 is 2, there can be no room for growth or imagination. To allow us some wiggle room we will instead focus on the interaction of generalized unknown quantities of currency. Through this approach we will develop recognizable patterns of operation in mathematics that can then be applied to specific arithmetic problems. This approach to mathematical problems is very useful and mastery of the subject is recommended. So without further delay, let us delve into the first mathematical operation of addition.

Addition is the process of combining two or more chains of currency into a single stack. The mathematical community has adopted the '+' symbol to indicate addition. Thus two strings of currency can be added by writing:

$$a + b = x$$

The above equation states that the variable a and the variable b will combine to form the total sum of x. Some readers may recognize that we have already encountered addition earlier in the chapter. Consider for a moment how the positive number tower was constructed. We first began with 1 square of currency and then introduced another square of currency to create the number two. This could have been written mathematically as:

$$1 + 1 = 2$$

Then we added another square of currency to produce another equation:

$$2 + 1 = 3$$

Or recognizing that two is actually one plus one we could write this as:

$$1 + 1 + 1 = 3$$

And so on and so forth until we reached infinity. The operation of adding one to a number may seem too simplistic to offer us any appreciable understanding of mathematics. Yet within these equations lay a very powerful general rule. Let's take a deeper look at what's happening. The first equation, adding one to one, is a symbolic representation of adding two unit stacks of currency together. Drawing this out pictorially would create:

Figure 1.13 – Addition of 1 plus 1

Notice that all we have done is taken the second unit and placed it atop the first unit to produce our answer of two. Moving on to the illustration of the second problem we would fine:

Figure 1.14 – Addition of 2 plus 1

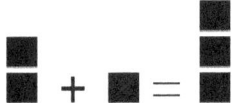

Again the process of addition is shown to be a stacking of the addends of 2 and 1 together to produce our solution of three. Thus our conceptual rule for addition is to simply take the stacks of currency that make up the addends and place them into a single stack. With this in mind we could easily tackle an addition problem such as:

$$2 + 3$$

To solve this we revert back to our illustration of two and three as stacks of currency:

Figure 1.15 – Addition of 2 plus 3

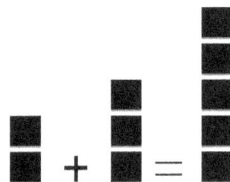

On inspecting the right hand side of the equation, we can easily see five squares of currency stacked together. Thus our answer for the addition of 2 and 3 is 5, easy enough. Conceptually, addition is not a very taxing operation. We simply place the addends into a single stack. The sum will be whatever the resulting height of the combined stack is.

Let's ignore actual numbers for now and instead focus on the opening equation for this subsection:

$$a + b = x$$

Although we have no idea what any of these variables are worth, we can still conceptually add them together by the tenets of addition. To do this, let us look at the governing pictorial representation:

$$a + b$$

Figure 1.16 – The Addition of a Plus b

The use of ellipses in the picture informs us that we are not quite sure how large the variable a or b is. Yet, there is other information that is readily available. First, notice that stack 'b' is taller than stack 'a'. Throughout this text, if a stack of currency is taller than another stack in the same illustration then we may go ahead and assume that it contains more currency. Generally this is not a valid assumption, but we will simplify things by allowing this notion. Second, we can also state that the two variable stacks are positive numbers since they are shaded squares. Because of this second piece of information, we can simply follow the pattern found while dealing with the numerical examples above. We will simply stack b on top of a. doing this provides 'x', the answer to the sum.

$$a + b = x$$

Figure 1.17 – Solution for the Sum of a Plus b

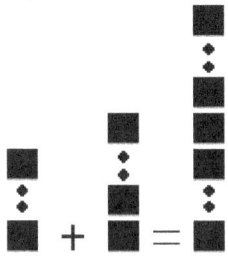

Likewise we used the process of addition to create the negative number tower as well. We simply used debt currency instead of the wealth currency.

$$(-1) + (-1) = -2$$

Where parentheses have been used to make sure we understand that two debt currencies have been added together. Once this was completed we then added another square of debt to the mix bringing us to a worth of negative 3. We would write this mathematically as:

$$(-2) + (-1) = -3$$

Pictorially it would look like this:

Figure 1.18 – Addition of Negative Two and Negative One

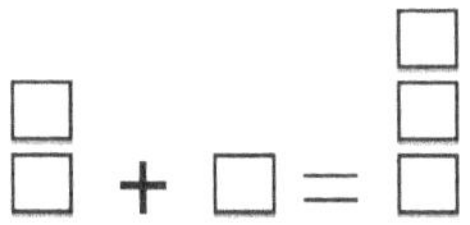

And we continued this process all the way until negative infinity. Thus without much effort we have successfully seen a way to add stacks of debt together, by simply placing one stack atop the other. With this in mind we could allow the two addends to be any negative number and still perform the same process of combining the two strings together into a single entity.

$$(-a) + (-b) = -x$$

Figure 1.19 – Addition of Negative a Plus Negative b

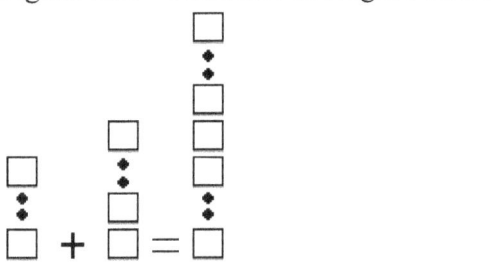

Hence, we have shown that addition of similar currency stacks is performed by combining the addends into a single stack.

Muscling our way through addition has left an obvious question to explore; what would happen if we were to add a string of debt currency to a string of wealth currency? Let's start out easy with only one unit of wealth and one unit of debt before progressing to larger quantities. Mathematically we would write

$$1 + (-1) =?$$

And the corresponding illustration:

Figure 1.20 – Addition of One Plus Negative One

$\blacksquare$ $+$ $\square$ $=$?

At this point we will introduce an axiom. An axiom is a rule or idea that is not argued to be true but given to be true. It is an idea that is only taken for granted and listed as a definition that governs a particular operation. The axiom under consideration presently states that wealth is used to satisfy debt. This means that one unit of debt added to one unit of wealth will result in the mutual destruction of both. With both of the currencies destroyed, we will be left with nothing. Luckily we have already defined nothing in mathematical terms: zero. Consequently, the addition of one unit of wealth with one unit of debt results in zero.

Equation 1.2
$$1 + (-1) = 0$$

But why restrict ourselves to numbers? Couldn't we use the same reasoning to show that any equal amounts of debt and wealth would reduce to zero? Of course we could. Mathematically and pictorially we would have:

Equation 1.3
$$n + (-n) = 0$$

Figure 1.21 Addition of n Plus Negative n

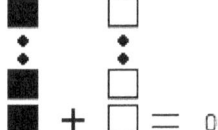

Because the two stacks are of equal height, we can assume that the two stacks contain an equal number of currencies. The only difference between the two stacks rests in the fact that one is composed of wealth while the other contains debt. Thus adding the two stacks would result in a one to one destruction of the debt and wealth currency ultimately leaving nothing left. But this solution brings up another concern. What would happen if we were to add unequal amounts of debt and wealth? To explore this new consideration let's define two variables amounts, shown below, that we will call D and E

Figure 1.22 – Addition of D and E

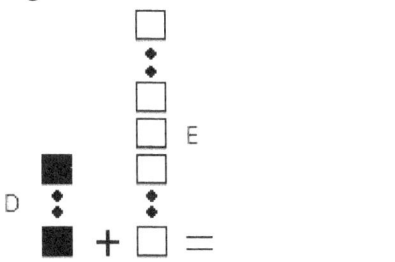

Notice that although we don't know the specific amount each variable represents, we can still make a few inferences about the variables. First notice that D contains wealth currency and E is composed of debt currency. This can be determined by whether the squares are shaded or unshaded. Notice that we have defined a positive variable to represent a negative number. This is not an uncommon occurrence in mathematics and one would do well to remember this as we progress through the text. Furthermore we can tell that E is larger than D because the currency stack is higher. I said larger rather than greater because D is a positive number and therefore 'greater than' E no matter how tall E may be.

Although the two stacks of currency aren't equal, we could easily break E into two subsets, one part of E that is equal to the entirety of D, and the other part composed of the leftovers.

Figure 1.23 – Illustration of Separating E into Two Groups

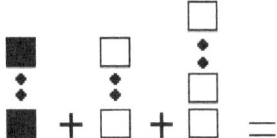

Mathematically we could write this as:

$$D + E_1 + E_2$$

At this point we can use the wealth of D to eliminate the 1st subset of E which will result in zero.

$$D + E_1 + E_2 = 0 + E_2$$

Figure 1.24 – Addition of D Plus E

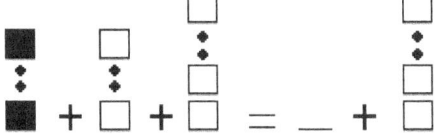

And of course we can see that adding zero bits of currency on top of the second partition of E won't increase the stack at all.

Equation 1.4
$$0 + E_2 = E_2$$
This logic goes further than the present particular problem. We can use the same argument for any amount of currency added to zero with the same logical conclusion necessarily following. We call this type of argument a general solution because it is relevant for all cases provided we meet the assumptions of the argument. (In this case, our assumption is that a number is defined by the height of the stack of currency)

Thus, when adding negative and positive numbers let the smallest stack erase out an equal portion of the larger stack. Whatever is left is your answer.

Section 1.5 - Commutative property of Addition

Addition contains an interesting property called the commutative property of addition. This property states that the order of the addition does not matter. To illustrate this consider that we would like to add D and E (the two variable strings of currency detailed before) together again. Before we wrote this as:

$$D + E = D + E_1 + E_2 = E_2$$
Now we would like to switch the order of the two variables and see if this changes anything. In other words we will rewrite the equation as:

$$E + D$$
Pictorially we will have:
Figure 1.25 – Addition of E Plus D

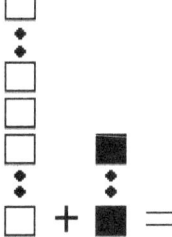

Notice that even though we switched the order of the two variables, the amount of positive and negative squares of currency remains the same. Since we haven't changed the problem in any appreciable way we shouldn't change the process for the solution. Hence we simply break E into two subsets, one equal to D, and eliminate the necessary. The resultant will still be whatever is left over. Thus both approaches are equal and the order has been shown to be immaterial.

Equation 1.5
$$E + D = D + E$$
Equation 1.5 is known as the commutative property of addition. This argument is a general solution for all addition and can be applied at will.

Section 1.6 - Subtraction

Addition was the process of combining arbitrary chains of currency together into a single group. Subtraction, on the other hand, deals with removing a given amount of currency from an original stack of currency. In this sense it can be interpreted as the inverse operation of addition.

Let us define two new variables F and G, pictured below.

Figure 1.26 – Illustration of F and G

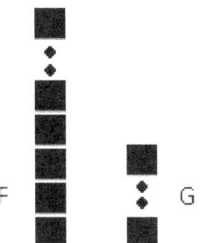

It should be obvious that both F and G are positive and that F is larger than G so we won't actually come out and state this explicitly…

Suppose we wish to subtract G from F, we would write this mathematically as:

$$F - G$$

Note that subtraction is symbolized by the dash, much like the negative number, and that it is the inverse of addition, much like debt is the inverse of wealth. This observation may pave a way to a very important mathematical property.

Without further meddling, subtracting G from F results in the removal of the height of G from F. This occurs because the value of G is determined by the height of the stack it represents and by removing the height of G from F we are removing the value of G from the value of F

Figure 1.27 – Subtraction of F minus G

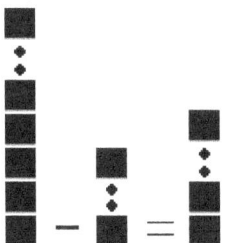

$$F - G = X$$

We will define the solution to this subtraction to be X. Remember the height of X because it will come into play later.

Now that we have accomplished the subtraction, let us define another stack of currency with the following conditions. First, that the stack of currency is comprised of debt currency. Second, that the height of the new stack is exactly the same as G.

Figure 1.28 – Variable G and the New Stack

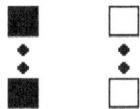

Since the new stack possess the same height as G, but made up of negative currency, then we will call this new variable negative G or (-G).

Now let us carry out the addition of F with negative G. Following our prescribed process detailed in the last section we will simply combine the two variables by removing an equivalent amount of F.

Figure 1.29 – Addition of F and Negative G

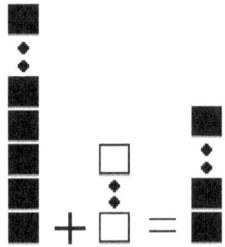

$$F + (-G) = X$$

This result shouldn't be surprising since both problems require a reduction in F by a worth of G. Thus we have shown that subtraction is a special case of addition. When we subtract we are really adding the negative.

Equation 1.6

$$F - G = F + (-G)$$

But what would happen if we were to subtract a negative number? I'm glad you asked. Let us now subtract the variable E, defined in the last section, from F.

$$F - E$$

Recall that we defined E, a positive variable, as a negative amount of currency. Thus mathematically we would simply follow the prior procedure and add the negative.

$$F - E = F + (-E)$$

And since positive E is comprised of debt currency, it stands to reason that negative E would be comprised of wealth currency. Mathematically this would mean that a negative amount of debt is actually positive:

Figure 1.30 – The Variable E Followed by the Variable Negative E

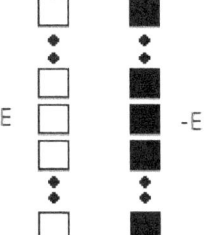

In other words, taking the negative of a stack of debt currency results in a positive number

Equation 1.7
$$-(-n) = n$$
Thus by our logic subtracting wealth results in a net loss of value, but subtracting debt results in a net increase of value.

Figure 1.31 – Equality of F Minus E and F Plus Negative E

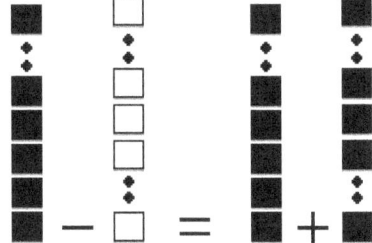

This should match our intuition and serve as a gut check because removing a portion of wealth is completely opposite of removing a portion of debt. Even though I have appealed to your intuition to verify our logical finding this does not mean we can use our intuition to produce results. We are only using our experiences as a check on our thought process to give us a warm tummy feeling that our results are consistent with real world phenomena. There will, however, be times that our logic seems to defy experience at first glance but will later prove to be true. More on this later.

With this piece in mind we can see that all subtraction can be defined by addition. Thus any rule we found to be applicable to addition will be applicable to subtraction… once we write the subtraction in the form of addition that is. For example, let's take the commutative property of addition from equation 1.5

$$E + D = D + E$$
We can easily apply this to the addition containing a debt currency like so:

$$F + (-G) = (-G) + F$$
But we would run into trouble if we used the commutative property on pure subtraction like this:

$$F - G \neq G - F$$
We could show why this would be inconsistent pictorially, but it would be far better for our mathematical logic skills to simply show why with symbols. Let us first write the subtraction of

G from F, and it's equivalent form in addition, and then write the subtraction of F from G, as well as it's equivalent form of addition.

$$F - G = F + (-G)$$
$$G - F = G + (-F)$$

Notice that the top equations equivalent addition is composed of a positive F and a negative G, while in the bottom equation we are adding a positive G and a negative F. Thus the result cannot be exactly the same because we are essentially adding completely different amounts of wealth and debt currency. Adding 1000 dollars of wealth to 5 dollars of debt is much different than adding 1000 dollars of debt to 5 dollars of wealth. Thus subtraction only follows the rules of addition when it is converted into its corresponding addition format.

Section 1.7 Numerical Examples:

Example 1.1 – Add 2 units of wealth to 3 units of wealth.
  - To begin, let's construct a picture of the two currency stacks

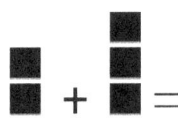

  - Since both stacks are of the same type, we simply place one atop the other and count the number of units. One should count five units total, thus 2 plus 3 is five.

$$2 + 3 = 5$$

Example 1.2 – Combine the numbers 2 and -4 through addition
  - To help us visualize the problem, let's again illustrate both stacks of currency

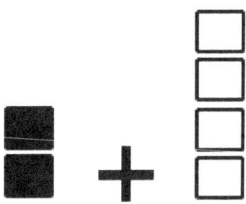

  - One should notice that the first stack is composed of wealth currency while the second stack is debt currency. By our assumptions covered in the chapter, we must use the wealth to satisfy the debt until one of the stacks are completely exhausted
  - Since the debt stack of currency is larger than the wealth stack, we can immediately tell that the wealth will be drained before the debt.
  - Thus measuring and equal amount of debt and wealth that will mutually destroy each other we are left with 2 units of debt that overcomes the wealth:
  - As can be seen, the result of 2 plus a negative 4 is 2 units of debt. Mathematically this can be written as:

$$2 + (-4) = -2$$

Example 1.3 – Perform the following operation: 5 – 4
  - This example requires us to subtract a positive number from another positive number.

- As argued in equation 1.6, to subtract a positive number you must add the negative. Rewriting the statement to reflect this new understanding

$$5 - 4 = 5 + (-4)$$

- Our new statement has the same form as the last example, so we may do well to approach it in the same way, destroying one unit of wealth for every unit of debt until one stack is eliminated.

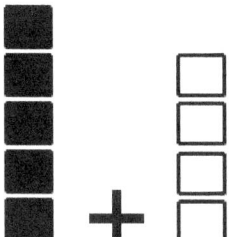

- Since the positive stack is larger than the negative stack, it will outlast the debt currency. Thus once all of the debt is eliminated we will be left with 1 unit of wealth.

$$5 + (-4) = 1$$

- And since our new statement is equal to our original statement then we could likewise write:

$$5 - 4 = 1$$

Example 1.4 – Perform the indicated operation.

$$3 + 2 - 5$$

- This example contains three separate numbers, positive 3, positive 2, and negative 5.
- Even though we have only been dealing with adding two numbers at a time, this shouldn't cause too much distress. We simply add the first two and then apply that result to the last number.
- Concentrating on the first pair of numbers we seek to add 3 and two together. Eschewing the picture this time around, we will visualize a stack of currency 2 units high combining with another stack of currency 3 units high. Together the new total height is five units
- Thus we can include this new information into our equation to find:

$$3 + 2 - 5 = 5 - 5$$

- Of course subtraction can be written as adding a negative, so let's also change that portion.

$$5 + (-5)$$

- Referring to equation 1.3, we notice that adding a positive stack of currency to the same height of debt currency will result in zero. Thus our final answer for the equation is zero.

$$3 + 2 - 5 = 0$$

Chapter 2: Multiplication

Section 2.1 – Definition of Multiplication

Consider some repeated accumulation of currency that occurs over time. For example, this could be a mortgage payment, a salaried pay-check, an annuity, or any other means of reliable and timely money transfer. We don't really care what the motive behind the transaction is, we only care that the payment is repetitive and of the exact same value. Our aim is to track the size of a currency stack as more and more transactions are processed and then see if any logical observations can help us later on.

As such we will begin with the first installment of currency and call this group d.

$$d$$

Figure 2.1 – The Variable d

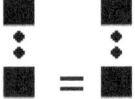

After the proper amount of time passes another installment of d is added to the account.

$$d + d$$

Figure 2.2 – Addition of d Plus d

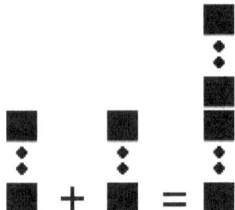

Again, the proper time passes and yet another installment of size d is added.

$$d + d + d$$

Figure 2.3 – Addition of d Plus d Plus d

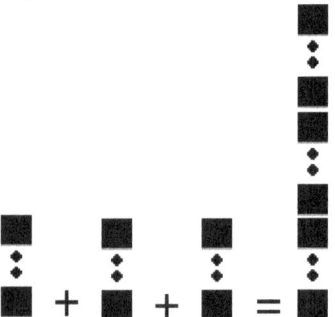

This process continues as more installments are piled one upon the other with each passing time period. Thus our stack of currency will continually grow like so.

$$d + d + d + d$$
$$d + d + d + d + d$$
$$d + d + d + d + d + d$$

I will forgo the pictorial representation as I trust the reader gets the idea. But even without the picture t process can become a little overwhelming to the point where we begin to lose track of how many installments have been applied. Does the last line contain 7 or 8 d's? It's hard for me to tell. Mathematicians strive for easier and more efficient ways of doing things and adding the same number repeatedly isn't something we, as mathematicians, would like to waste time on. To circumvent this problem mathematicians have developed the short-hand notation of multiplication. To use multiplication we simply count how many repeated groups of addition are present and list that number directly before the variable. Observe:

$$d + d = 2d$$

Notice that we do not use a symbol to indicate multiplication. We merely list the number and then the variable. If we wanted to multiply two variables then we would simply write the two variables together. In the case of two numbers, we would use parenthesis around one or both of the numbers. We do not use the 'x' symbol for multiplication unless we are talking about 3 dimensional multiplications, a topic that is extremely interesting but not very useful for our purposes. Extending this logic of multiplication to three groups of d added together we find:

$$d + d + d = 3d$$

Or just as easily we could define 4 groups of d added together to be:

$$d + d + d + d = 4d$$

Or just as easily we could write n groups of d added together as:

Equation 2.1
$$d + d + \cdots + d = nd$$

The ellipsis in the mathematical statement above was encountered last chapter and instructs us to continue the obvious pattern. The obvious pattern being to repeatedly add another d until the nth d is accounted for. Equation 2.1 provides a method of writing long strings of repeated addition concisely for any finite number n and can be viewed as the definition of multiplication.

This new value, nd, should still be interpreted as a unique value of its own. It is composed of the separate variables n and d to be sure, but the definition of numbers we accepted in the previous chapter simply stated that a number represented a certain height of currency; which nd does. Of course we don't know exactly how high the number nd is. But that shouldn't stop us from defining nd as a positive number since it is made up of positive stacks of currency.

Moving on, we seek to expand the understanding of multiplication to include repeated groups of addition of debt currency. Starting out just as before, we begin with one instance of debt:

$$(-d)$$

Figure 2.4 – The Variable Negative d

Letting another installment of negative d transpire gives us:

$$(-d) + (-d) = 2(-d)$$

Figure 2.5 – Addition of Negative d Twice

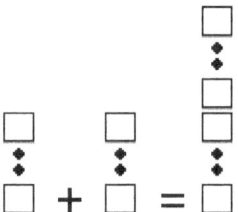

Obviously we are simply repeating the same argument as before for positive numbers. We can plainly see that adding repeated groups of debt currency will produce the same notation.

$$n(-d) = (-d) + (-d) + \cdots + (-d)$$

One could interpret this continual addition of negative numbers as a continual rise up the debt number tower. Thus we could argue that the result of this operation of adding repeated negative numbers will itself be negative. But let's also not forget that the height of negative d is exactly the same as positive d, they only differ by the type of currency they are composed of. Thus n groups of negative d will have the same height n groups of positive d and we can label this new quantity as the negative of the result before.

Equation 2.2

$$n(-d) = -(nd)$$

This equation shows that a negative number multiplied by a positive number of groups will result in a negative number.

This, and every other result obtained so far, has resided within the realm of experience. No matter what we have argued or derived, we have always returned to our intuition as a check for the validity of the result. Yet the power of mathematics resides in its ability to describe the indescribable, to explore the unexplorable, and define the undefinable. So let's experience the unexperienceable. What if we tried to posit negative groups of addition of wealth currency? The mathematical statement would look like this:

$$-n(d)$$

How can we possess negative groups of anything? Could you, for instance, hold negative 30 gold coins in your hand? Of course not, but luckily for us mathematics doesn't necessarily care what is physically possible. So let's explore another property that could pave a way for us to interpret negative groups of addition.

Section 2.2 – Commutative property of multiplication

One interesting aspect of multiplication is that a number can be written as repeated groups of unit addition, or integers. Consider the number two for instance:

$$2 = 2(1) = 1 + 1$$

Which we already know to be a definition of 2 because that is exactly how we constructed the number two in the last chapter. We can press on by defining 3 in terms of multiplication as 3(1), and four as 4(1). In fact our general rule is any number multiplied by one is by definition that very number. Mathematically we write that:

Equation 2.3

$$n(1) = n$$

But what if we were looking at this equation the wrong way. What if we instead wished to list this as 1 group of 2, or 1 group of 3, or 1 group of n units of currency? Well, by the definition of multiplication, if we only had one group present then we would presently have one full group.

$$1(2) = 2$$
$$1(3) = 3$$
$$1(n) = n$$

And consequently, since both interpretations give us the same answer, we can equate the two different scenarios like so:

$$n(1) = 1(n)$$

Or if we would instead use a variable amount instead of 1 we would find:

Equation 2.4

$$nd = dn$$

This states that n groups of d added together has exactly the same value as d groups of n added together. This is a very curious property if you truly stop to think about it. In essence this means that 47 groups of 93 are exactly the same as 93 groups of 47. This may not be readily believable so for further illustration let's consider some product of two numbers, say 3(5) = 15. Now let's recall that 5 is actually 5 groups of 1 and that 3(5) means 3 groups of 5 added together. With this information let us construct the following illustration:

1 1 1 1 1
1 1 1 1 1
1 1 1 1 1

As we already know, 3 rows of 5 added together is a total of fifteen, which is exactly what we have proven in the illustration. But couldn't we also interpret this in terms of columns rather than rows? In that case we see that we have five columns of three which also equals 15. In fact any multiplication can be set up in this manner and the commutative property of multiplication is shown to be logically consistent.

One very interesting application of the commutative property stems from trying to prove what zero groups of a number would be. Consider the following:

$$0d$$

By the definition of multiplication this would mean zero groups of d. Since zero is defined as nothing then zero groups must infer nothing groups. No groups would mean the space is empty so that would be our answer, nothing or zero. Admittedly, this wouldn't be a bad intuitive guess. But we need to shy away from our intuition and use actual mathematical rules to prove our ponderings. For instance, we could use the commutative property of multiplication to rewrite the statement as:

$$0d = d0$$

Using the definition of multiplication at this point we can easily interpret this as d groups of 0 added together. Mathematically it would look like this:

$$d0 = 0 + 0 + \cdots + 0$$

Recall that the sum is defined by the height of the stack along the number tower. But adding nothing, no matter how many times, will never cause an increase in height. Thus we can say without qualm that repeatedly adding zero will result in zero. Therefore, anything finite number multiplied by zero will be zero.

Equation 2.5

$$0d = 0$$

This result did happen to match our intuition, but be aware that we will be soon be encountering a few arguments that go against our first impressions. But since our intuition was correct, we might as well run with it. We could further expand the definition of zero groups to include negative numbers as well. Consider the following statement:

$$0(-d)$$

With the understanding that zero groups means nothing is there, we can define zero multiplied by a negative number to be zero as well.

$$0(-d) = 0$$

Another interesting application of the commutative property of multiplication stems from the repeated addition of debt currency. For instance, consider the multiplication of 3 and (-5), which by our understanding can be stated as three groups of negative five added together equaling (-15). Using the fact that negative five is five groups of negative one, and following the same process as before we can show that three rows of negative five can be arranged like so:

(-1)(-1)(-1)(-1)(-1)
(-1)(-1)(-1)(-1)(-1)
(-1)(-1)(-1)(-1)(-1)

But again, we could also interpret this illustration to be five columns of (-3) which can also be shown to be negative fifteen. This shows that the commutative property of multiplication works for positive groups of negative numbers as well.

$$3(-5) = (-3)5$$

Because all multiplication has been shown to be commutative, we can now explore a mathematical statement that stumped us earlier. Recall that we couldn't logically explain negative groups of addition because we don't know what negative groups are. To place ourselves on firmer logical footing we will use the commutative property of multiplication as applied in equation 2.4 above to transform the statement:

Equation 2.6

$$(-n)d = n(-d)$$

Now we can easily see that n negative groups of d added together is the same as positive n repeated groups of negative d. Through this method we have successfully sidestepped the problem of negative groups of addition and shown that it is mathematically equivalent to repeated groups of subtraction.

We could use this new understanding to further define the connection between positive and negative numbers. Consider using equation 2.3 to write negative two as:

$$-2 = 1(-2)$$

Now using our newest tool, equation 2.6 we can rewrite the right hand side as:

$$1(-2) = 2(-1)$$

By the definition of multiplication we could write this as:

$$2(-1) = (-1) + (-1)$$

And we have come full circle. This is exactly how we constructed negative numbers in the first place, by adding units of debt currency. Although we haven't encountered any new territory with this exploration, we still received a welcome verification that our work so far is consistent. With this understood, it is no great leap of logic to then define any negative number, represented by (–n), as:

Equation 2.7

$$-n = n(-1)$$

But multiplying negative groups of a positive number was too easy. Let's make it a little more difficult, just for fun. Let's approach negative groups of debt. This could be written mathematically as:

$$-n(-d)$$

In this case, even if we used the commutative property, we would still have the original problem of not being able to describe negative groups. Since we cannot give a compelling argument we could try listing an axiom, but that would not be the mathematician's way. Mathematics strives to find compelling arguments for truths rather than just taking someone's word for it. So jealous is this quest that there are only a few axioms allowed in mathematics. As such, we should wait until we are a little more experienced before we try to tackle this problem.

Section 2.3 – Multiplying groups of addition:

Consider a repeated summation of accounts. This could be a result of working two salaried jobs or perhaps two bills that must be met each month. Whatever the specific reason, we have a mathematical statement like the following:

$$d(e + f)$$

This statement is known as the distributive property of multiplication over addition (henceforth referred to simply as the distributive property) and is a very powerful algebraic tool. It will open many doors for us in the future and needs to be understood fully. To approach the distributive property in the gentlest of way, let's first make d = 1, e any account positive or negative, and f any account value positive or negative. Writing our supposals together we have:

$$1(e + f)$$

We have already defined that anything multiplied by one is itself as shown in equation 2.3 above. So this answer was a gimme, 1 group of e + f is simply the statement e + f.

$$1(e + f) = e + f$$

Notice (and this is a very important point) that we cannot combine e and f into the shorthand of multiplication because they are not repeated groups of addition. Moving on, let's set d = 2 and see what comes about.

$$2(e + f)$$

Under our understanding of multiplication, this statement calls for 2 groups of (e + f) added together. Following this interpretation in the basest sense we find:

$$2(e + f) = (e + f) + (e + f)$$

The right hand side of the equation can be interpreted as a summation of a summation. Thus all rules of addition are valid on the right hand side of the equation. Using the commutative property of addition, we can swap the middle f and e to produce the following statement:

$$e + f + e + f = e + e + f + f$$

Using the definition of multiplication we can now simplify this into our desired form

$$2e + 2f$$

Moving on we set d = 3 and then expand that into three groups of (e + f).

$$3(e + f) = (e + f) + (e + f) + (e + f)$$

Under the same assumptions presented before, we can successively use the commutative property of addition to rewrite the right side of the equation into a more useable form:

$$e + e + e + f + f + f$$

Finally we can again use the definition of multiplication to combine the repeated summation into a simplified result.

$$3(e + f) = 3e + 3f$$

We could continue this until we are blue in the face and never cover every situation. So let's try and find a logical pattern associated with our previous arguments. Listing our general formula as:

$$d(e + f)$$

Let's deduce what would happen if we were to logically carry out the same process as before but with d groups of addition. Notice that the variable d designates how many groups of the parenthesis are present in the statement once it is written out in the long form. That is to say, when d was 1 there was only one group of e plus f. When d was 2 then there were two groups of e plus f. So we can state mathematically that when d is d then we will have d groups of e plus f added together.

$$(e + f) + (e + f) + \cdots + (e + f)$$

At this point we simply maneuver all of the e's together and all of the f's together through the logic of the commutative property of addition to find:

$$e + e + \cdots + e + f + f + \cdots + f$$

The question now is, how many e's and f's populate our statement? This is easily answered because there was only one e and one f in each of the d groups of parenthesis. Thus there is a one to one ratio and we can easily say that d groups of e and d groups of f populate the current statement. With this in mind we can formally define the distributive property.

Equation 2.8
$$d(e + f) = de + df$$

Be aware that we could also reverse the process. If we instead started the equation with a string of addition containing a common multiplication then we could remove that common multiple outside of a parenthesis like so:

$$de + df = d(e + f)$$

This is logically sound by the congruence property of the equation. Since we have proven that one statement logically follows from another, then we can 'equally' say that the other statement logically follows the first. We will be actually using this reverse of the distributive property in more situations than the original distributive property.

Now that we have shown that d could be distributed through a parenthesis with two variables, it is a trifle to show that it doesn't matter how large the parenthetic statement is, you simply multiply every term by the account outside the parenthesis. Mathematically it would look something like this.

Equation 2.9
$$d(e + f + g + h + \cdots) = de + df + dg + dh + \cdots$$

And of course, since it is defined by addition, we can apply the distributive property to a subtraction as well, assuming we have written the subtraction in terms of addition. This distributive property is very powerful because it will be used as a logical step in many of the derivations we will be performing. As an illustration of its power, the distributive property can even solve the problem we recently ran into; the double negative multiplication.

Section 2.4 - Double Negative Multiplication

A lot of you may already know the solution to a double negative product but lack a compelling reason to believe it. This is unacceptable as far as mathematics is concerned because if you can't convincingly argue why something is true then you haven't really understood it. Remember that we are trying to objectively comprehend the workings of interest, not merely reflect how we, or how our teachers, feel it should work.

Multiplication of two negative numbers will look like so:

$$(-n)(-d)$$

Using the definition of a negative number in equation 2.7 we can separate each of the negative numbers into the corresponding variable multiplied by negative one.

$$(-n)(-d) = (-1)(n)(-1)(d)$$

Using the commutative property of multiplication we can then reorder the four items into:

$$(-1)(-1)(n)(d)$$

Since we have already have a firm understanding of (n)(d) then we only need to focus on the first two items being multiplied together. To simplify this process, let's equate the negative one multiplied by negative one to some variable x.

$$(-1)(-1) = x$$

This is perfectly legal since x is just a variable and by definition an unknown value. We now seek to impose a value upon x that we can, through the power of equality, define to be the result of a double negative multiplication. The first step in this derivation is to use the additive property of zero to the left hand side of the equation.

$$(-1)(-1) + 0 = x$$

Notice that adding zero does not change the value of the equation at all as per our argument in equation 1.4. Moving cautiously forward, we shall recall that one plus a negative one is equal to zero as in equation 1.2. Since we have two statements that are equal (-1+1 and 0) we can then interchange them at will. Replacing the zero in the equation above with its equated statement gives:

$$(-1)(-1) - 1 + 1 = x$$

Now we will recall that subtracting a positive number is the same as adding a negative number, thus the negative one can be changed to:

$$(-1)(-1) + (-1) + 1 = x$$

Then rewriting the negative one as a product of negative one and positive one, as shown in equation 2.7

$$(-1)(-1) + 1(-1) + 1 = x$$

At this point, we can use the distributive property in reverse to remove a negative one from the first two multiplications on the left hand side of the equation.

$$(-1)(-1 + 1) + 1 = x$$

Notice that if we were to redistribute the negative one back into the parenthesis we would still have the exact form of the previous statement. Thus this maneuver does not change the value of the equation. In fact, at any point we could logically reduce each statement to return to our original conjecture that (-1)(-1) = x.

Focusing on the large set of parenthesis of the equation above we should see a negative one plus a positive one. Recall that equation 1.2 stated that adding equal heights of wealth and debt together will result in zero. Thus we can replace the (-1 + 1) with zero.

$$(-1)(0) + 1 = x$$

Recall further that anything finite multiplied by zero is zero by equation 2.5. Thus negative one multiplied by zero is still zero.

$$0 + 1 = x$$

Now we only need to recognize that adding zero to anything results in itself, as argued by equation 1.4. Thus the left hand side of the equation is simply one.

$$1 = x$$

Now that we have defined the unknown variable x, we can equate this with the original statement and see that a negative one multiplied by a negative one is a positive one.

Equation 2.10
$$(-1)(-1) = x = 1$$

As we will recall, this mirrors our findings in the last section for equation 1.7 when we said that the negative of debt currency is wealth currency.

$$-(-n) = n$$

So we again find a connected result through two different means. This gives us further backing that we are traveling down a consistent path.

Section 2.5 – Even and odd numbers

An even number is defined as an integer that is a multiple of the number two. This means that we could construct an even number by multiplying some integer b with two.

Equation 2.11
$$even = 2b$$

An odd number is defined as any even number plus one. Thus because an even number is defined as 2b, and odd number is defined as:

Equation 2.12
$$odd = 2b + 1$$

Of course if we added one more unit of currency to an odd number we would then arrive at an even number again. Observe

$$2b + 1 + 1 = 2b + 2$$

Then we could use the distributive property in reverse to pull out the common two.

$$2b + 2 = 2(b + 1)$$

And since we now have a number that is written as a product of two and some parenthetic integer, we have another even number by definition. Yet an odd number does not have this same property because we cannot use the distributive property to pull out a common two. This creates an interesting dichotomy between the various integers. They are either even or odd, and never both.

Section 2.6 – Division:

There is a counter operation for every mathematical operation. For addition it was subtraction. For multiplication it is division. The transition into division from multiplication has an obvious impetus. Consider some multiplication of two numbers that produce a resulting value.

$$nd = x$$

Which we can interpret as n groups of d added together to produce the value of x. Throughout the previous sections it was assumed that n and d were both known values that could be combined to produce a value for x. We now put the other shoe on so to speak. Let's assume that we know the value of x and the value of n, but haven't a clue what d is. How will we find the value of d in this situation?

One method to determine the value of d is a process known as division. Division posits how large an individual group would be if a value was separated into a specified number of equal groups. In our example above, this would mean that we seek to distribute the value of x into n different groups. The value of one of these groups would be the solution to our unknown variable d. Mathematically we write this as:

$$d = \frac{x}{n}$$

Which states that d is equal to x divided by n. In this statement x is in the numerator (the top) and is termed the dividend, the number being divided. The variable n is called the divisor and is located in the denominator (the bottom). To pictorially illustrate division, let us define x to be some large stack of debt currency and n to be 2. Dividing x by 2 would result in sectioning the tower representing x into two new stacks, each exactly half the size of the original.

Figure 2.6 – Division of x by Two

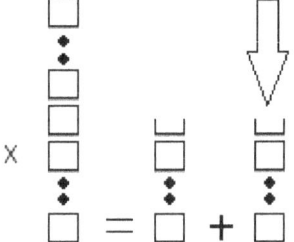

The size of one of the half-size stacks is the value of d, marked by an arrow. We could easily do the exact same thing for the case where n equals 4. Performing the same process pictorially we would have:

Figure 2.7 – Division of x by Four

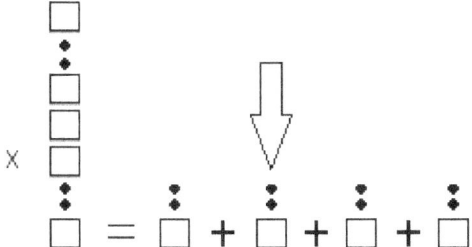

And again the size of d would be represented by one of these new smaller stacks with an arrow. What is important to understand though is that the process would be the same regardless of the actual size of n. We would simply distribute the entirety of x into n equal but distinct groups and then measure the size of one of these new groups to label it d – our solution.

Now that we have the understanding of division down conceptually, we would be well rewarded to explore a few special cases. The first we special case we will scrutinize is division by itself. Mathematically it would look like:

$$\frac{x}{x} = d$$

Let's try to reason this problem to conclusion without the aid of a pictorial representation. However, I will invite you to attempt to 'see' how the abstract argument would play out in your mind's eye. Let us imagine that we encounter an arbitrary tower of currency with a measurement of x units of currency in height. (Note that I did not specify wealth or debt currency as our argument does not depend on which we choose) Our goal is to separate this tower into exactly x equal stacks of currency. Now, since the height of the tower is determined by stacking x unit currency squares atop each other we could easily say that the tower is comprised of x groups of single unit currencies. Thus without much stress we have partitioned the height of the tower into x groups of one, the answer to d!

Equation 2.13

$$\frac{x}{x} = 1$$

Another special case is dividing by an arbitrary variable by one. Mathematically this would look like:

$$\frac{x}{1} = ?$$

Again, we shall try to logically argue the necessary value without the aid of pictures. In fact, one should get used to this type of mathematics as many important concepts cannot easily be illustrated and instead rely on the readers ability to improve upon previous concepts. Our division problem above asks us to distribute the value of x into one equal group… but isn't the number itself already in a single group? Therefore we are already finished. The whole of the variable has been distributed to one group and is given by the entire number. Mathematically we conclude:

Equation 2.14

$$\frac{x}{1} = x$$

Another special circumstance for division we will identify is the case of division by zero. Division of any finite account by zero will look like this:

$$\frac{d}{0}$$

There is an inherent logical fallacy associated with this mathematical statement because division looks to distribute the numerator into an equal number of groups specified by the denominator. But notice that the amount of groups we will use in this case is zero. So how can we distribute a stack into zero groups? The short answer is we can't. As such the division definition breaks down when we try to divide by zero. We say that any finite account divided by zero has no solution.

Equation 2.15

$$\frac{d}{0} = no\ solution$$

Trying to divide by zero creates an inconsistency in logic that painfully shows the shortcomings of algebra. But where there is uncertainty, there is often times opportunity. Mathematicians tried to develop ways to get around the inability to divide by zero. For their efforts calculus was born. I would sincerely suggest finding a book on calculus because the entire modern world is based upon it. This book will not approach calculus as we are more concerned with understanding interest. But once you master this book I wholeheartedly recommend studying calculus. Once calculus is understood, then more advanced notions of interest can be easily explained and conquered.

The last special case we will explore in this book is division by a negative number. Mathematically it would look like:

$$\frac{x}{-n} = d$$

Unfortunately our interpretation of the definition of division produces utter nonsense in this configuration because we cannot specify what a negative group would be. One should remember, however, that we encountered this exact conundrum when dealing with negative groups in multiplication. Our solution entailed sidestepping it entirely by using the commutative property to show that negative groups of a positive number could be interpreted as positive groups of a negative number. Thus one might wish to see if division could support the commutative property as well and solve our problem in a similar manner.

So, does the order matter in division? Could we switch the variables from top to bottom while maintaining the statements value? Unfortunately no, we can't. To show this quickly we will use the example:

$$\frac{2}{1}$$

By equation 2.14 we have already proven this to be equal to two. To test the feasibility of the commutative property we simply switch the position of the two numbers to produce:

$$\frac{1}{2}$$

The statement above would instruct us to separate one unit of currency into two groups, which we should be able to recognize as one half. It shouldn't be too much of a surprise to know that one half is not the same as two units. Thus division fails to contain the commutative property and we are at an impasse.

Yet, there is one other option we haven't explored yet. One will recall how subtraction could be defined within addition by equation 1.6. Through this concept we were able to apply the commutative property to subtraction even though pure subtraction failed to conform to the needed assumptions. This then begs the question; could we do the same with division?

2.7 Defining division within multiplication.

Recall that multiplication is defined as the addition of repeated accounts. When we write 2d we mean two groups of d combining together through addition. When we write nd we mean n groups of d added together. Of course we also had 0d, meaning there were no groups of d, and 1d which meant one group of d was present. So what would happen if we wrote:

$$\frac{1}{2}d$$

We could easily extend the definition of multiplication to interpret this as meaning a half group of d. But one will recall that we have developed an alternative notation for a half group of d, namely dividing d by 2.

$$\frac{d}{2}$$

So through this basic argument we have discovered a way to write the same process two different ways. In this way we can now assume to define division within the realm of multiplication.

Equation 2.16

$$\frac{d}{c} = \frac{1}{c}d$$

If we accept this interpretation of division then all of the logical rules that govern multiplication can also be applied to division, as division is only a special case of multiplication through this understanding. Since multiplication is commutative, we could also interpret division as being commutative through equation 2.16

$$\frac{1}{c}d = d\frac{1}{c}$$

And by the definition of multiplication we can now write what was division as a string of addition.

Equation 2.17

$$d\frac{1}{c} = \frac{1}{c} + \frac{1}{c} + \cdots + \frac{1}{c}$$

It would not be a great stretch to include some repeated variable in the numerator and then suggest that repeated groups of addition of a given ratio would follow the exact same rules.

$$\frac{w}{c} + \frac{w}{c} + \cdots + \frac{w}{c}$$

Assuming we had d groups of this repeated ratio we could easily rewrite the statement with the shorthand of multiplication:

$$d\left(\frac{w}{c}\right)$$

Then using equation 2.16 we could combine the d into the numerator:

Equation 2.18

$$d\left(\frac{w}{c}\right) = \frac{dw}{c}$$

One special consideration of equation 2.18 above happens when d = c. Substituting this value into the equation gives:

$$\frac{dw}{c} = w\left(\frac{d}{d}\right)$$

Which we have already shown to be 1 by equation 2.13.

Equation 2.19

$$\frac{dw}{d} = w(1) = w$$

As can be seen, allowing division to be defined within multiplication opens many logical doors for us to use during our quest for the interest bearing mathematics.

Section 2.8 – Division by a negative number

Now that we have defined division by multiplication, we can attack the problem that gave us pause.

$$\frac{x}{-n} = d$$

By rewriting the equation in terms of multiplication we have:

$$x\left(\frac{1}{-n}\right) = d$$

Now we can clearly see that we have x positive groups of the number one over negative n. But as in equation 2.6, it is well understood that multiplication can switch the negative sign from one portion of the product to another. With this property in mind we can move the negative sign to the top of the ratio instead of the bottom without loss of the equality.

Equation 2.20

$$\frac{x}{-n} = \frac{-x}{n}$$

Of course, should we encounter a double negative division such as:

$$\frac{-x}{-n}$$

Then we could still invoke the multiplicative format which will pave a direct path to canceling the negative signs as shown in equation 2.10

$$-x\left(\frac{1}{-n}\right) = (-1)(-1)x\left(\frac{1}{n}\right) = x\left(\frac{1}{n}\right)$$

Thus a common negative may be divided out just as any common variable

Equation 2.21

$$\frac{-x}{-n} = \frac{x}{n}$$

Section 2.9 – Compound division

Consider the following mathematical statement that we will define as compound division.

$$\frac{\left(\frac{a}{b}\right)}{c}$$

We seek a simplification of the statement into a single divisor line. First, by using our definition of division within the realm of multiplication we will find:

$$\frac{a}{b}\left(\frac{1}{c}\right)$$

The ratio of a divided by b has already been defined. It is a separating of the height of a into b separate, but equal, groups. Since we already know how to interpret this ratio, let's treat it as a variable in its own right with its own specific, but unknown, height illustrated in the picture below.

Figure 2.8 – Division of a by b

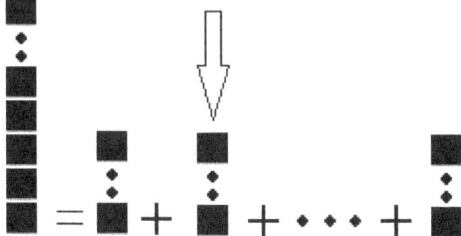

Now that we have defined the height, or value, of the ratio a/b it is a trifle to further subdivide that value into c equal groups. The height of one of the newly separated groups will be the result of the full operation as detailed by the illustration below.

Figure 2.9 – The Division of a by b and Further Divided by c

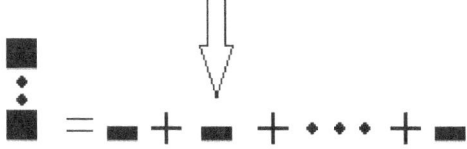

Conceptually speaking, we have figured out how to interpret how the compound division will behave. Unfortunately, we have still not figured out a way to write the statement with a single divisor line. To do this we will use the fact that we have separated the ratio of a/b's height into c distinct groups. But, one will remember, that the height of the ratio was first determined by separating the variable a into b separate groups. In essence we are only cutting up one of the b groups into c subsections. So what would happen if we instead were to apply the c subcuts to all b groups that make up a? Adding up the total cuts throughout the whole of the original value a we would find:

$$c + c + \cdots + c = bc$$

Because there will be c cuts for each of the b groups of a! Thus we could say that when we divide the variable a by b and then c successively, we are really dividing the variable a by the product of bc.

Equation 2.22

$$\frac{\left(\frac{a}{b}\right)}{c} = \frac{a}{bc}$$

Or more generally, writing the right hand side as a multiplication:

$$\frac{\left(\frac{a}{b}\right)}{c} = a\frac{1}{bc}$$

But let's continue to play around with equation 2.22 to see if we can't find another useful tidbit. For instance, what would happen if we first wrote equation 2.22 in terms of multiplication.

$$\frac{\left(\frac{a}{b}\right)}{c} = \frac{a}{b}\frac{1}{c}$$

Then also rewrote the ratio a/b in terms of multiplication as well.

$$\frac{a}{b}\frac{1}{c} = a\frac{1}{b}\frac{1}{c}$$

Since we have performed reversible and equal operations at each stage, then we know that this result must be equal to the result obtained in the equation above.

$$a\frac{1}{b}\frac{1}{c} = a\frac{1}{bc}$$

Thus multiplying two divisional terms, 1/b and 1/c, results in a product of the two denominators:

Equation 2.23

$$\frac{1}{b}\frac{1}{c} = \frac{1}{bc}$$

This will prove to be useful in further chapters as we shall see.

Section 2.10 – Numerical Example:

Example 2.1 – multiply 2 by 3
- Mathematically this can be written as:

$$2(3)$$

- Recall that multiplication is defined as repeated groups of addition.
- This problem can be interpreted as two groups of three added together.

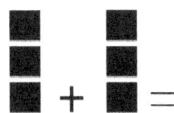

- By our understanding of addition, we combine the two heights and then count the number of units, which gives us the number 6.
- Thus the result of our multiplication is 6

$$2(3) = 6$$

Example 2.2 – Multiply the following: 2(3)(2)
- Although this example contains three numbers multiplied together rather than the usual two, we shall see that it behaves in exactly the same manner as before.
- One way to interpret this procedure can be given mathematically as:

$$2[(3)(2)]$$

- Which means that we have two groups of addition of the bracketed statement 3 times 2.

$$[(3)(2)] + [(3)(2)]$$

- Because multiplication is commutative, as shown by equation 2.4, we could actually use the results from example 1 and state that both brackets are equal to 6.

$$[6] + [6]$$

- Now it's a simple matter of adding the two sixes together through the tenets of addition.
- Our result should be 12.

$$2(3)(2) = 12$$

- Another route to this answer is to simply multiply the first two numbers

$$2(3)(2) = 6(2)$$

- Then multiply the result by the next number

$$6(2) = 12$$

- This latter method is useful as the amount of numbers needing to be multiplied together increases.

Example 2.3 – Perform the needed operations:

$$2\frac{2}{-4}$$

- One method to approach this problem is to use equation 2.16 to rewrite the ratio as multiplication:

$$2(2)\left(\frac{1}{-4}\right)$$

- Now we can multiply both twos together

$$4\left(\frac{1}{-4}\right)$$

- Rewriting the multiplication in terms of division again we find:

$$\frac{4}{-4}$$

- Some readers may have trouble visualizing negative four groups, so we can use equation 2.20 to move the negative sign to the numerator.

$$\frac{-4}{4}$$

- Now it's a simple task of dividing a stack of debt currency four units high into four equal groups, the result is four groups of one unit of debt. Thus our result is negative one.

$$2\left(\frac{2}{-4}\right) = -1$$

Example 2.4 – distribute the 2 across the parenthesis

$$2(x + 3)$$

- Using equation 2.8 we can easily multiply each term inside of the parenthesis by 2.

$$2x + 2(3)$$

- The first part of the summation, 2x, is considered simplified because we can't write it any more concisely. The last part however, 2(3), can be written as single number. Performing the multiplication we find:

$$2x + 6$$

Example 2.5 – Perform the following division

$$\frac{\left(\frac{12}{2}\right)}{3}$$

- This form of division was covered in equation 2.22 and was referred to as compound division

- Thus we can rewrite this equation as:

$$\frac{12}{2(3)}$$

- Multiplying the two numbers in the denominator results in:

$$\frac{12}{6}$$

- Using the definition of division as a separation of the numerator into an amount of groups determined by the denominator, we see that we need to separate 12 units of currency into 6 groups
- Doing this produces 2 units of currency in each group
- Our solution is therefore 2

$$\frac{\left(\frac{12}{2}\right)}{3} = 2$$

Chapter 3 - Exponents

Section 3.1 – Defenition of Exponents:
Multiplication was defined in the last chapter as a way to write repeated addition in a concise manner. Expanding upon this premise, we wonder what would occur if we encountered repeated multiplication. The answer to this quandary rests in the mathematical operation of the exponent, and it is developed like so:

Consider some mathematical process that requires multiplying a variable by itself on a repetitive basis. The first instance of this occurrence may look like:

$$xx$$

And the next multiplication would then consist of:

$$xxx$$

And the next:

$$xxxx$$

And so on and so forth until we reach some large repetitive multiplication of our variable.

$$xxxxxxxxxxxx$$

One should notice that this repetitive multiplication can easily overwhelm the reader when trying to count the number of variables present within the above string of multiplication. What we need is a shorthand method of tallying the number of existing repeated multiplications just as we developed for multiplication. To do this, we will adopt the traditional method of an exponential statement consisting of a base, the number being multiplied repeatedly, and the exponent, written as a superscript superseding the base, which represents the number of repeated groups of multiplication. Thus an exponent, or power, of n would signify n groups of multiplication:

Equation 3.1
$$x^n = xxx \dots x$$

Since an exponent of n represents n groups of multiplication, what would an exponent of 1 signify? Well, by the definition of the exponent, one group of x would be one group of x. Written formally this would be:

$$x^1 = x$$

Thus x standing by itself is equal to… x. This was not very surprising and many of the readers could have guessed this statement. So let's move on to the next logical step: the second power

$$x^2 = xx$$

Because a two in the exponent means that we have two groups of x multiplied together. Obviously we could go further still in our definitions and show that:

$$xxx = x^3$$
$$xxxx = x^4$$
$$xxxxx = x^5$$

And so on and so on. Thus the exponent shouldn't be too hard to understand. We simply multiply the base by itself a repeated number of times specified by the exponent.

Since we are now experts at the exponent, it shouldn't be too difficult to interpret something like the zeroith exponent. Mathematically it would be written as:

$$x^0$$

Well, by the definition of the exponent, zero groups of x would be… nothing. Since we have already defined nothing to be zero, then x raised to the zeroith power must be zero! This may seems like a perfectly legitimate argument, but it is completely wrong. A variable raised to the zeroith exponent is not zero. But don't take my word for it. In fact, don't take my word for anything in mathematics because I don't make the rules. I may ask permission to take a few facts for granted, or I may guide a logical argument to a 'traditional' conclusion here and there, but I am by no means a governing authority on mathematics. The only way you should accept the conjecture that the zeroith exponent is not zero is by me providing a convincing argument that it isn't.

So let's begin the journey to provide a solid argument for the zeroith exponent.

Section 3.2 – Product Rule:

Consider a multiplication of two exponential statements with the same base.

$$x^L x^K$$

If possible, we would like to write this product as a single exponential statement. Since we have never approached this type of statement before, let's begin with something we know to be true.

$$xx = x^2$$

We know that the above statement is true by the definition of the exponent. Pushing a little further we will multiply the result by another x.

$$x^2 x$$

Substituting the definition of x to the second power into the equation above we will find:

$$x^2 x = (xx)x$$

Which, one will recall, is the definition of x raised to the 3rd power

$$xxx = x^3$$

Thus multiplying x raised to the second power by another x will result in x raised to the third power. If we continued this pattern of multiplying an x with the previous result then we would find:

$$x^3 x = (xxx)x = x^4$$
$$x^4 x = (xxxx)x = x^5$$
$$x^5 x = (xxxxx)x = x^6$$

Notice that no matter how large an exponent we start with, multiplying another x into the mix will result in an exponent one unit larger. This should make sense since we are by definition introducing one more group of multiplication. Thus if we were presented with L groups of multiplication and we introduced yet another x we would have:

$$x^L x = (xxx \dots x)x = x^{L+1}$$

So the next logical question would be: what would happen if we increased the exponent of the second multiplier? To start out, let's increase this exponent to two and see what happens

$$x^L x^2 = (xx \dots x)(xx)$$

The L groups of repeated x is joined by exactly two groups of multiplication when multiplied by x raised to the second power. Thus we can say with ease that the total amount of x present in the statement is whatever L is and two more.

$$x^L x^2 = x^{L+2}$$

With this basic understanding of the logic we can continually increase the exponent of the second variable until we are comfortable enough to state the 'obvious' pattern.

$$x^L x^3 = (xx \dots x)(xxx) = x^{L+3}$$
$$x^L x^4 = (xx \dots x)(xxxx) = x^{L+4}$$
$$x^L x^K = (xx \dots x)(xxx \dots x) = x^{L+K}$$

The last line of the argument secures the desired operation. This states that two exponential statements of the same base multiplied together results in the addition of the exponents. It is not important to remember the last sentence word from word, but rather to remember the logic behind the argument that produced the statement. In this way we are focused on the Interaction of logical arguments rather than the rote memorization of unconnected statements. Formalizing the findings:

Equation 3.2

$$x^L x^K = x^{L+K}$$

Notice that this product rule of exponents is only valid for the same base variable. If we wished to multiply exponential statements that consist of varying bases then the product rule would not be applicable. To appreciate the difference let us list the definition of a multiplication with different bases.

$$x^L y^K = (xx \dots x)(yy \dots y)$$

Since the definition of an exponent only covers repeated multiplication of the same base then these two groups of multiplication cannot be combined into a single group. As such the product rule fails in this circumstance as shown.

Section 3.3 – Power of a product rule

The power of a product seeks to find a corresponding statement that is equal to the following mathematical statement:

$$(a^k b^L)^n$$

Following the same format we used to create the product rule, we will first set n=1 and then increase the magnitude to see if we can make any logical observations. Thus our first mathematical statement would be:

$$(a^k b^L)^1$$

Notice that raising a statement to the first power corresponds to one group of multiplication. In other words one group of the quantity inside the parenthesis is itself, the quantity within the parenthesis.

$$(a^k b^L)^1 = a^k b^L$$

Setting n equal to 2 results in two groups multiplied together.

$$(a^k b^L)^2 = (a^k b^L)(a^k b^L)$$

At this point, we can use the commutative property of multiplication to rearrange the above statement into:

$$(a^k b^L)(a^k b^L) = a^k a^k b^L b^L$$

We should notice that the above statement contains two instances of repeated multiplication, two groups of a and two groups of b. Thus we can use the exponential notation to re-write the statement as:

$$a^k a^k b^L b^L = a^{k+k} b^{L+L}$$

And look, we now have repeated groups of addition within the exponent. Thus if we used the definition of multiplication we could show that the exponent could be written as:

$$a^{k+k} b^{L+L} = a^{2k} b^{2L}$$

And now we can formally equate the starting statement with the final statement to produce:

$$(a^k b^L)^2 = a^{2k} b^{2L}$$

Moving on, let's increase the value of n to 3, and following a very similar argument as when n equals 2 we will find:

$$(a^k b^L)^3 = (a^k b^L)(a^k b^L)(a^k b^L)$$
$$= a^k a^k a^k b^L b^L b^L$$

Notice again that we have used the commutative property of multiplication to rearrange the equation so that we have repeated groups of multiplication in regards to first a and then b. Re-writing the equation with exponential notation and setting it equal to the original statement produces:

$$(a^k b^L)^3 = a^{3k} b^{3L}$$

We could continue this pattern for larger and larger exponents ad nauseum, but let's stop for a minute and try to tease out the underlying principles of the process. First, notice that the magnitude of the exponent dictates how many groups of multiplication are contained within the statement.

$$(a^k b^L)^n = (a^k b^L)(a^k b^L) \dots (a^k b^L)$$

Thus we have n groups of the parenthetic statement all multiplied together. Since we are dealing with pure multiplication, and since multiplication is commutative, we are then allowed to rearrange the equation with the complete set of the first variable a followed by the complete set of the second variable b.

$$= a^k a^k \dots a^k b^L b^L \dots b^L$$

Finally since we have repeated groups of multiplication of the variable a and the variable b then we can write the rearranged statement in exponential notation. Recalling that we had a total of n groups of both a and b produces:

Equation 3.3

$$(a^k b^L)^n = a^{nk} b^{nL}$$

Thus, no matter how large (or small) the exponent of the parenthetic statement, each variable inside the parenthesis will be multiplied by itself a number of times determined by said exponent. Notice that this only works because we are dealing with pure multiplication. If we wished instead to raise a sum to an exponential power then we couldn't follow the same path.

$$(a + b)^n \neq a^n + b^n$$

We can't distribute the exponent into the parenthesis like before because addition and multiplication are not logically equivalent. To see this we write out the meaning of the above statement without exponents.

$$(a + b)^n = (a + b)(a + b) \dots (a + b)$$

But don't see this exercise as a failure because we will use this interpretation extensively once we finally focus on interest.

Section 3.4 – Quotient rule

Consider the division of an exponential statement by another exponential statement of the same base variable. Mathematically it would look something like this.

$$\frac{x^n}{x^L}$$

Our goal is to find a concise and applicable rule that could simplify this situation. To find this rule it is best that we first start out with an easy example. Let's consider what would happen if we were to divide x squared by x.

$$\frac{x^2}{x} = \frac{xx}{x}$$

This must be true since x squared is defined as two groups of x multiplied together. At this point we could easily divide out the common factor of x in both numerator and denominator as we demonstrated in equation 2.13

$$\frac{xx}{x} = x\frac{x}{x} = x(1) = x$$

Thus we have reduced the exponent of the dividend by eliminating a common base from the top and bottom. Let's expand upon this example and once we are comfortable with the process try to procure a useful pattern. Setting the numerator to x raised to the third power would create:

$$\frac{x^3}{x} = \frac{xxx}{x} = xx\frac{x}{x} = x^2$$

This argument follows exactly the same logic as before. We first wrote the exponential statement as groups of multiplication and then divided out the common factor of x. Increasing the power of the numerator once more and repeating the logical argument we find:

$$\frac{x^4}{x} = \frac{xxxx}{x} = xxx\frac{x}{x} = x^3$$

By now we should notice the basic idea that the x in the denominator is eliminating one of the x from the numerator. This results in the reduction of the numerator's exponent by one. One might argue that no matter how many x were contained in the numerator the process would remain the same. One x from the numerator will be eliminated by the x in the denominator and we would have one less x than we started with in the numerator. In other words, if we started with n groups of x in the numerator and divided out a single x, then

$$\frac{x^n}{x} = x^{n-1}$$

And our resulting exponent would contain one less than the original n. With this under our belt we turn our attention to increasing the amount of x contained in the denominator to see if we can't find some recognizable pattern as well. Consider dividing x to the nth by x to the second:

$$\frac{x^n}{x^2} = \frac{x \ldots xxxx}{xx}$$

Notice that the only thing that has changed from the previous argument is that we now have two x in the denominator. Thus we will simply pair each x in the denominator with an x in the numerator like so:

$$\frac{x^n}{x^2} = x \ldots xx\frac{xx}{xx}$$

Now, by using equation 2.13 to reduce the fraction to one we will find:

$$\frac{x^n}{x^2} = x \ldots xx$$

As can be seen, all we have to do is count all of the groups of x to specify the exponent in the final simplification. Unfortunately, we don't know the exact number of x being multiplied together because we didn't explicitly state how many we had started with. All we know is that n stands for some generalized number. But the beauty of mathematics is that we don't have to know, we can simply express this new number as n – 2 because we had n originally, whatever that may be, then took two away from that total. Thus given any n to begin with, we will be left with all of the n groups except 2.

$$\frac{x^n}{x^2} = x^{n-2}$$

Increasing the denominator one more time produces:

$$\frac{x^n}{x^3} = \frac{xxxx \ldots x}{xxx} = x \ldots x\frac{xxx}{xxx}$$

Again we see the opportunity to divide out a common term from both numerator and denominator three times. Rewriting the simplification with an exponent we find:

$$\frac{x^n}{x^3} = x^{n-3}$$

At this point we have found a dependable pattern. The denominator will divide out as many x as it can from the numerator until there are no more x in the denominator. Thus if we had L repeated multiplications in the denominator, we would simply subtract L from n, giving us our final answer. Mathematically this will look like:

Equation 3.4

$$\frac{x^n}{x^L} = x^{n-L}$$

Section 3.5 – Zero Exponent:

Consider the following statement

$$x^0$$

Unfortunately, as mentioned before, there is no direct and obvious physical interpretation for an exponent of zero. One could posit that, because exponents describe how many repeated groups of multiplication are present, a zero exponent would mean that no groups are there. That person would be correct at this point, but he would be incorrect to then state that, intuitively, no repeated groups are the same as zero. Although a convincing argument, and one I must admit I fell for when I was learning, this would be wrong because it wouldn't be consistent with the new tools we have developed. Mathematics is a game of logic, not intuition. It doesn't matter how much we feel it in our heart, bones, or other body parts, we can only use what has been shown to be true as stepping stones to what has not otherwise been shown. One just such potential stepping stone is the quotient rule from equation 3.4

$$\frac{x^n}{x^L} = x^{n-L}$$

The ability to parlay the quotient rule into a zeroith exponent stems from a judicious choice of L. What would happen if we let L be equal to n? Mathematically substituting n for L in equation 3.4 gives:

$$\frac{x^n}{x^n} = x^{n-n} = x^0$$

And out pops the culprit. So now we just have to figure out what x to the nth divided by x to the nth is equal to. But haven't we already proven this in Chapter 2? Recall that equation 2.13 dictates that any finite variable divided by itself is 1.

$$x^0 = \frac{x^n}{x^n} = 1$$

Thus we can state clearly that x raised to the zeroith power is one.

Equation 3.5

$$x^0 = 1$$

Certainly this was a surprising result and one to dwell on. But one should be cautioned that this rule does not work for x equal to zero. We will not encounter anything like that in this text, but if you were to use it in other applications, you must remember that you can't divide by zero in algebra.

Section 3.6 – The radical

In the first chapter we developed subtraction as the counter operation to addition. The second chapter introduced division as a counter operation to multiplication. We now seek a counter operation to the exponential statement, which we will term the radical. Consider an exponential statement of the form:

$$x = y^{\frac{1}{n}}$$

This ratio in the exponent is termed a radical. It instructs the reader to counter the operation of the exponent. This means that we seek to, figuratively, repeatedly multiply y by itself an nth amount of times. Notice that this doesn't mean 'n' times, but 'nth' times, one over n amount of times. This of course causes quite a problem because we can't count an 'nth' amount of times on our fingers. Luckily for us though, mathematics is not concerned with whether we can actually count one nth, only that we can describe it.

Let's first assume that the radical exponent is consistent with all of the exponential rules derived in this chapter. If you grant me this assumption, then let's also raise both sides of our radical to a power of n. Doing this produces:

$$(x)^n = \left(y^{\frac{1}{n}}\right)^n$$

The last step is perfectly logical because if the two sides are equal to begin with, then multiplying both sides by itself n times will give us the exact same number, maintaining the equality. Using the results of equation 3.3, and our assumption that the radical behaves like an exponent, we can write our argument as:

$$x^n = y^{\frac{n}{n}}$$

Now, by the use of equation 2.13 we can reduce the ratio in the exponent to one, giving us:

$$x^n = y$$

This means that the radical statement is just another way to write an exponential statement! Thus we can interpret the nth radical of y to be the number that equals y when multiplied by itself n times. This definition may seem confusing at first glance, but numerical examples will be provided to solidify the understanding.

One side note to be aware of is that there is no real solution to a negative number with an even root (meaning n is an even number in the equation above). Luckily for us, all necessary roots in the type of interest accumulations we will be studying only require the positive bases, thus we will simply define all instances where roots are taken to be positive and won't need to consider negative bases or outcomes. Those students who are interested in what will result if we took an even root of a negative number could examine texts on complex numbers, a truly exciting subject with such whimsical notions as imaginary numbers, polar coordinates, and color wheel graphs.

Section 3.7 – Numerical Examples

Example 3.1 – Simplify the following expression

$$(3^2 4^3)^3$$

- The exponent can become very unwieldy very quickly. As such it is usually better to simplify the exponent before we attempt to perform the multiplications
- Using equation 3.3 to distribute the exponent across the parenthesis

$$3^6 4^9$$

- I recommend using a calculator for the actual multiplication, but one should remember that we are multiplying six groups of three and then nine groups of four
- Six groups of three is equal to 729, and nine groups of four is 6561
- Thus inserting these equivalent values into the mathematical statement we have

$$729(6561)$$

- Our last step is to perform the multiplication

$$4782969$$

- As can be seen, seemingly small numbers can combine through the exponent to culminate in millions

Example 3.2 – Simplify the following expression

$$\left(\frac{35xz^{18}}{2\Delta n[p]} + \frac{\partial x}{\beta q} - 3\right)^0$$

- This problem is quite complex and will take an expert hand to solve it, to this we turn our attention
- Notice that the entire mathematical statement is raised to the zeroith power.
- Assuming that everything within the parenthesis is finite, we can utilize equation 3.5
- Thus the result is one

$$\left(\frac{35xz^{18}}{2\Delta n[p]} + \frac{\partial x}{\beta q} - 3\right)^0 = 1$$

- Easy enough

Example 3.3 – solve for x

$$x = 9^{\frac{1}{2}}$$

- This exponent contains a ratio, meaning that it is actually a radical exponent.
- One could easily take the second radical in a calculator, but it would be very useful to see the connection between radicals and exponents

- Let's instead use the equivalent exponential form of the radical as argued in section 3.6

$$x^2 = 9$$

- Now what number multiplied by itself twice is equal to nine? After some searching we notice that multiplying 3 by itself does indeed equal 9

$$3(3) = 9$$

- Thus we can state with confidence that the second radical of 9 is 3

$$9^{\frac{1}{2}} = 3$$

Example 3.4 – solve for y

$$y = 15^{\frac{1}{3}}$$

- Again we have a ratio in the exponent which signifies a radical
- First rewriting the equation as argued during the radical section.

$$y^3 = 15$$

- Some readers may be tempted to say that y must equal 5, but they would be wrong!
- Recall that the exponent is involved with repeated groups of MULTIPLICATION, not addition
- Although it is true that adding 5 three times will equal 15, it is not true for 5 multiplied by itself three times, that would equal 125.
- It turns out that no matter how much we search, we cannot find a specific number that can be multiplied by itself three times and equal 15
- However, and this is very important, that doesn't mean it doesn't exist!
- The best we can do is to estimate the answer to the third radical of 15 as:

$$15^{\frac{1}{3}} = 2.466212074 \ldots$$

- I didn't personally arrive at this answer, I simply truncated the result my calculator provided.
- This means that multiplying a number close to 2.466212074 by itself three times will actually be 15.
- As can be seen, radicals can become quite a handful in their own right. But one should get used to seeing answers like this in the world of interest calculations.

Example 3.5 – Simplify the following:

$$(3^3 3)^{\frac{1}{4}}$$

- Our first step is to rewrite the parenthesis in terms of an exponent. Notice that three to the third is 3 groups of 3 multiplied together. Multiplying one more three into the mix will raise the total number of groups to 4, thus:

$$(3^4)^{\frac{1}{4}}$$

- Now using the power of a product rule, we can place the radical into the exponent section

$$3^{\frac{4}{4}}$$

- Notice that 4 divided by 4 is one as shown in equation 2.13

$$3^1$$

- And we have already defined 3 to the first power as 3. Therefore our solution to the equation is 3.

$$(3^3 3)^{\frac{1}{4}} = 3$$

Example 3.6 – Simplify the following:

$$\frac{2^{10}}{2^5}$$

- Using equation 3.4 we can rid ourselves of the ratio

$$2^{10-5}$$

- Performing the subtraction yields:

$$2^5$$

- Multiplying 2 by itself 5 times results in 32

$$\frac{2^{10}}{2^5} = 32$$

- Not so bad once you get down to it.

Chapter 4: Logarithms

Section 4.1 – Introduction to Logarithms

In the last chapter we found a way to interpret an exponential statement such as:

$$x^n = y$$

Through this statement we observed that we could find the value of y by multiplying x by itself a total of n times. If we instead did not know a value for x, but had the value of y and n, then we could use the radical property to mathematically represent the value of x as:

$$x = y^{\frac{1}{n}}$$

With the exponential and radical statement we could mathematically represent a value for either x or y. But yet there is one glaring omission in our mastery of the exponential statement; the exponent itself. At this time we do not possess a tool to solve for an unknown exponent.

One method developed to represent the value of an exponent is known as the logarithm. The logarithm represents the same information as an exponential statement but in a different format, much like the radical notation was shown to be. Given the exponential statement at the beginning of this chapter we can write the corresponding logarithmic notation as:

$$\log_x y = n$$

To pronounce this mathematical statement you would say 'log base x of y equals n'. It was no mere coincidence that we said 'base x' because x is the base number for the exponential variable n. Conceptually, the logarithm asks how large of an exponent n is needed for the repeated multiplication of x to equal the whole of y. The important thing to note, however, is that no new information has been presented through the logarithm. It is simply another way to write the exponential statement.

The logarithmic notation can be confusing at first. But memorization of the maxim 'log base of answer equals exponent' can ease this transition. This little statement means that if I was looking at an exponential equation and I wanted to write the logarithm I would first write 'log' and then whatever the base was in subscript, then the other side of the exponential equation, and then the equal sign, and finally whatever the exponent was. Although I don't usually like a student to engage in rote memorization in mathematics, I would advise you to remember 'log base of answer equals exponent'

Section 4.2 – The Natural Logarithm

An exponential statement can conceivably have any base, meaning x could be any number in the universe, and consequently so could the logarithm. Luckily for us though, we can restrict our attention to one logarithmic base for the rest of the text. This special base is known as the natural base and is represented by the constant e, an important number in mathematics. Let's introduce an exponential statement in base e.

$$e^n = y$$

The constant e is approximated to be 2.718, but there are more precise definitions of e which we will encounter later. Notice that we labeled e as a constant and not a variable. It represents a concrete value just like the symbols 10, 25, or 1.

The corresponding logarithmic notation with base e would be:

$$\ln y = n$$

The ln has been used to specify that we are dealing with the natural logarithm, a logarithm with base e. Here we have maintained our 'log base of answer equals exponent' with the understanding that ln is log base e.

Section 4.3 – Reflexive Identities:

The starting place for all of the rules of logarithms begins with two very obvious facts. First that an exponential statement is equal to itself:

Equation 4.1

$$e^x = e^x$$

And that the logarithmic statement is equal to itself:

Equation 4.2

$$\ln x = \ln x$$

We can use these two statements to produce the reflexive identities of logarithms. This is done by utilizing the two different ways of writing a statement, exponentially or logarithmically. For instance, let us take the exponential statement of equality and write it logarithmically.

Equation 4.3

$$ln(e^x) = x$$

Which follows the maxim, log base of answer equals exponent. (Notice that the right hand side of equation 4.1 was also e raised to the power x, thus it was our 'answer') This result tells us that if we take the logarithm of an exponential statement, with a similar base of course, we get the exponent. This should make sense intuitively because the logarithm seeks the number that the base must be raised to equal the 'answer'. Since the logarithmic base is e, then we obviously need to raise e to a power of x so that it can equal the value of e raised to the power of x regardless of the actual value of x. In other words we have the equation:

$$e^? = e^x$$

And we are trying to find what we can place in the question mark so as to have an equal statement. If we used x in place of the question mark, then we would have the reflexive property of equality detailed in chapter 1 and our problem would be solved. Now rewriting the above statement in logarithmic format we have 'log base of answer equals exponent'

$$\ln(e^x) = ?$$

Since we have already argued that the question mark is x, we have the exact same statement as equation 4.3. With this in mind we immediately turn our attention to the logarithm statement of equality.

$$\ln x = \ln x$$

To write this in terms of an exponential statement we must first define the parts of this logarithmic equation. One should repeat 'log base of answer equals exponent'. Thus we can call the entire right hand side of the equation as the exponent of the corresponding exponential statement because of the order of our maxim. This leaves only the left hand side of the equation to deal with. One will recall that the logarithm ln is defined to have the base e. Thus the base of the exponential statement must be e. By process of elimination x must then be the answer. Thus the equivalent exponential statement is:

Equation 4.4

$$e^{\ln(x)} = x$$

These two properties will be used extensively while exploring the properties of logarithms.

Section 4.4 – Addition of logarithms:

Assuming we are concerned with the same logarithmic base, we seek an equivalent statement to the addition of two logarithms. Mathematically it would look like this:

$$z = \ln(x) + \ln(y)$$

Our goal then, is to find a statement for z that will be logically equal to the right hand side of the equation. Our first step will be to place both sides of the equation into the exponent position.

$$e^z = e^{\ln(x) + \ln(y)}$$

This is allowable in mathematics because if the two sides are equivalent then they would produce the same equivalent exponent. Thus we are simply writing equation 4.1, the reflexive property of equality for exponential statements, in another form. Now that we have the equation in exponential form we can use equation 3.2 to separate the addition into two exponential statements

$$e^{\ln(x) + \ln(y)} = e^{\ln(x)} e^{\ln(y)}$$

By applying the results of equation 4.4 to both exponential statements on the right we will have:

$$e^{\ln(x)} e^{\ln(y)} = xy$$

At this point we should combine this simplified statement with the beginning left hand side.

$$e^z = xy$$

This statement is very similar to a pure exponential statement that started this section. Hence, it will be easy to isolate z by invoking the definition of the logarithm. Log base of answer equals exponent.

$$\ln(xy) = z$$

We have arrived at a new equivalent statement for z. By the powers of equality we can replace z with the right hand side of the equation above giving us our desired equivalent statement:

Equation 4.5

$$\ln(xy) = \ln(x) + \ln(y)$$

Section 4.5 – Subtraction of Logarithms:

Consider the following mathematical statement:

$$z = \ln(x) - \ln(y)$$

One may be tempted to say that since subtraction is within the realm of addition then the answer should follow the same format as the last argument. You would be correct to think this way, but instead of making bold, yet unfounded, statements we should simply let the math lead us. To begin, let's use the same trick we used when attacking the addition of logarithms. Let's place both sides in the exponential position.

$$e^z = e^{\ln(x) - \ln(y)}$$

Immediately we see a chance to use equation 3.4, the quotient rule of exponents. Invoking the rule provides:

$$e^z = \frac{e^{\ln(x)}}{e^{\ln(y)}}$$

Now we use equation 4.4 to rewrite the ratio in a simplified manner.

$$e^z = \frac{x}{y}$$

Now we simply use the definition of a logarithm, log base of answer equals exponent, and viola we have found a new way to write z:

$$\ln\left(\frac{x}{y}\right) = z$$

Formalizing our findings we write our result out as:

Equation 4.6

$$\ln\left(\frac{x}{y}\right) = \ln(x) - \ln(y)$$

Section 4.6 – The Power rule of logarithms:

Let us imagine a mathematical statement that contains an exponent within a logarithm, like so.

$$\ln(x^n)$$

By using the definition of exponents, we can rewrite the logarithm as:

$$\ln(xxx \dots x)$$

This statement shows n groups of x multiplied together. One should recall that we have already shown that a product inside a logarithm can be written as an addition of logarithms as in equation 4.5. Doing this gives:

$$\ln(x) + \ln(x) + \cdots + \ln(x)$$

Recall that repeated groups of addition can be written in the shorthand of multiplication. Since we had n groups of x multiplied together inside the logarithm we know that we now have precisely n groups of the logarithms added together. Thus we can rewrite this as a product of n and ln(x)

$$n \ln(x)$$

Formalizing by equating the beginning with the end of our argument we find equation 4.7, the power rule of logarithms.

Equation 4.7

$$\ln(x^n) = n\ln(x)$$

Section 4.7 – Numerical examples:

Example 4.1 – Solve the following provided ln(x) is equal to 5

$$\ln(x^4)$$

- We know the ln(x) is equal to 5, but our current statement contains x to the fourth power, which is not the same.
- How can we transform the statement into something we can use
- One way is to utilize equation 4.7 to rewrite the equation as:

$$4\ln(x)$$

- Now we simply substitute the information we were provided for ln(x) and we find:

$$4(5) = 20$$

- And we have successfully solved the example problem.

Example 4.2 – Find the following value:

$$\ln(5)$$

- As a general rule of thumb, it is best to approach the logarithm through a calculating device. That used to mean slide rules or log tables, but in our modern world most calculators can do the job.

$$\ln(5) = 1.60943\ldots$$

- If one feels that using a calculator is cheating then I completely understand their sentiment. I would then point them to the following equivalent equation

$$e^x = 5$$

- Keep in mind that e = 2.71828…
- Good luck!
- As for me, I'll use the calculator

Example 4.3 – Find the following:

$$\ln(100000)$$

- Plugging this into the calculator gives:

$$\ln(100000) = 11.5129\ldots$$

- As can be seen, a very large change in the value of the logarithm number corresponds with a relatively small change in the result

Example 4.4 – Find the following:

$$\ln(152)$$

- Plugging this into the calculator provides:

$$\ln(152) = 5.02388\ldots$$

Example 4.5 – Find the following x

$$\ln(-4) = x$$

- Plugging this into the calculator gives… wait I must have made a mistake… still won't work… maybe my calculator is broken… Still can't get this darn thing to give me an answer… what's going on?
- We could check our input into the calculator until we turn blue, the fact is that this is an invalid mathematical process. To find out why, let's write the logarithmic equation in terms of an exponent.
- Using our chant, 'log base of answer equals exponent', we know that the base is e, the exponent is x, and the answer is negative four

$$e^x = -4$$

- To further clarify our conundrum, let's write e in its decimal notation.

$$2.71828\ldots^x = -4$$

- Thus we seek the number of times we can multiply 2.71828… by itself to produce a negative number
- But 2.71… is a positive number, and multiplying two positive numbers produces another positive number by our definition of multiplication. Couple this with the process for multiplying large groups of multiplication as shown in example 2.2 and we will continually have a positive result
- Thus it is impossible for e to be multiplied by itself any number of times and produce a negative number
- This serves as reminder that the calculator is a tool, not a crutch. You can't rely on the calculator to do the actual mathematics, only to perform the tedious calculations.

Chapter 5 – Order of Operations

Section 5.1 – GLEMA
The governing equations of the interest bearing mathematics exist as an amalgamation of the operations considered so far. This presents a problem because our study has only considered one operation at a time. To progress further, we must understand the order of operations. The order of operations can be interpreted as the grammatical rules of mathematics as they set the ground rules for proper writing and reading of mathematics. Aptitude in this area is critical because the ability to adhere to these tenets of mathematical grammar ensures that our logical ponderings are understood long after we are gone.

Our level of mathematics only requires an order of operations that can be completely described within the acronym of GLEMA:

Grouping symbols – Parenthesis, brackets, divisor lines

Logarithms

Exponents

pure **M**ultiplication – Although division is defined within multiplication, a divisor line can act as a grouping symbol

Addition
This means that when evaluating a mathematical statement we must deal with each of the above groups in turn. All grouping symbols must be dealt with before we can move to logarithms, then exponents, then multiplication, and finally addition. However, the grouping symbols themselves may hold a complex assortment of operations up to and including other grouping symbols within them. And those may hold other grouping symbols, and so on and so on like a Russian nested doll. In this way the order of operations could operate on a tiered structure and the application can become complex.

Numerical examples will be provided at the end of the chapter as well as our usual theoretical explorations in the following sections to help solidify your understanding. To start with, let's look at the interaction of common terms.

Section 5.2 – Addition of Common terms
Consider the following addition:

$$x^n + x^n$$

Looking carefully at this statement, one might notice repeated groups of addition; the definition of multiplication. Rewriting this in the shorthand of multiplication produces:

$$x^n + x^n = 2x^n$$

Of course, we needn't stop at only two groups. We could easily generalize this idea by allowing b amount of groups of addition added together.

$$x^n + \cdots + x^n = bx^n$$

What we have just constructed in known as a term. A term is composed of the coefficient, base, and exponent. The variable b in this example would be known as the coefficient. The b could be a constant number, like the 2 to the left of the x in the equation before, but does not necessarily have to be and could be a variable in its own right. The x is known as the base variable because it is the base of the well-known exponent, n in this case. A term can be interpreted as a repeated addition of an exponential statement, as seen above. But one should be careful to make sure that it is actually a repeated addition. For instance, consider the following:

$$x^3 + x$$

Can we combine these two terms above through the shorthand of multiplicative notation? Of course not, because the exponents are not exactly repeated. Expand x raised to the third exponent to see this illustrated:

$$xxx + x$$

We cannot combine these two different expressions through multiplication because as numbers they are as different as x and y. Thus one may string multiple terms together that cannot be simplified as so:

$$ax^n + bx^{n-1} + cx^{n-2} + \cdots$$

This string of terms is considered simplified because none of these terms can be combined by the logic of multiplication

Section 5.3 - Multiplication of addition

Consider the following multiplication of summations

$$(a + b)(c + d)$$

One may be tempted to multiply before the addition, because M comes before A in GLEMA, but this would be incorrect. The parentheses act as a grouping symbol, which is contained in G, the first letter of GLEMA. Thus we must perform the addition within the parenthesis before we can multiply. Unfortunately, there is nothing more we can do mathematically in either of the parenthesis because an addition of two general variables is just that, an addition of two general variables and they cannot be simplified. But, what if we were to use the distributive property of multiplication into addition given by equation 2.8

$$e(c + d) = ec + ed$$

Obviously this type of distribution is valid provided that we take the entirety of (a + b) to act as a single variable. So why don't we? Why don't we let e in the statement above be the sum of a and b? Doing this allows us to distribute the equivalent parenthetic statement. This type of logical leap is exactly the sort I would like to see you make in mathematics. We took something we knew and applied it to what, at first glance, appeared to be a slightly different set of circumstances. Once we trained our mind to accept that a sum can act like a single variable then we can logically manipulate the equation as if we were dealing with a single variable. Doing this provides

Equation 5.1
$$(a + b)(c + d) = (a + b)c + (a + b)d$$

Now we could easily distribute both the c and the d into their respective parenthetic statement giving us four terms of addition.

$$ac + bc + ad + bd$$

The key here was to recognize that we could distribute a parenthetic summation in the same manner as a single variable. Of course we could extend the size of the distribution easily by writing.

$$(a + b)(c + d + e + \pi + \cdots)$$

Where again, we simply treat the sum (a + b) as a single variable and distribute it across.

$$(a + b)c + (a + b)d + \cdots$$

Then of course we could use the distributive property again to get rid of all parentheses. Since this concept is so easy, let's look at a special case. Consider the following mathematical statement.

$$(a + b)(a + b)$$

Yes, we could easily approach this in the same manner and distribute across parenthesis providing us with:

$$(a + b)a + (a + b)b$$

Then distributing again:

$$aa + ba + ab + bb$$

Finally we can utilize the exponential notation and combine like terms to present the result:

Equation 5.2
$$(a + b)(a + b) = a^2 + 2ba + b^2$$

But we would be missing a great opportunity to expand our definition of the exponent. Isn't the statement in equation 5.2 just repeated multiplications? Of course it is. Thus we could write:

Equation 5.3
$$(a + b)(a + b) = (a + b)^2$$

Or generalizing to any number of positive groups we would have:

Equation 5.4
$$(a + b)(a + b) \ldots (a + b) = (a + b)^n$$

As we can see, we can logically manipulate whole mathematical statements, not just variables, without skipping a beat.

Section 5.4 – Addition of Division

Even though division is defined within multiplication, there is a particular subset that gives many people problems in mathematics; the addition of fractions. The goal in adding fractions is to combine two ratios into one divisor line. To start off easy, let's approach two addends with the same divisor. Consider the statement:

$$\frac{a}{b} + \frac{c}{b}$$

Rewriting these divisions in terms of multiplication we will find:

$$a\frac{1}{b} + c\frac{1}{b}$$

At this point we could easily use the distributive property in reverse to pull out the common multiple of 1/b:

$$= (a + c)\frac{1}{b}$$

Now we have the opportunity to rewrite the equation back into division resulting in.

$$\frac{a + c}{b}$$

Viola, we have been able to combine two additive division terms into a single term. Formalizing we have:

Equation 5.5

$$\frac{a}{b} + \frac{c}{b} = \frac{a + c}{b}$$

This result will prove useful while powering our way through the mathematics of interest, but we have not finished yet. Let's make it a little more difficult and try an addition with different divisors. Consider the following mathematical statement:

$$\frac{a}{b} + \frac{c}{d}$$

Unfortunately, if we rewrote these two statements in terms of multiplication we wouldn't be able to pull out a common divisor because there is none. Observe:

$$a\frac{1}{b} + c\frac{1}{d}$$

But perhaps the method isn't flawed, only our approach. Let's use two other mathematical principals to help us out. The first is the multiplicative property of unity and the second is the divisional property of unity.

$$a(1) = a$$
$$\frac{d}{d} = 1$$

These two mathematical properties will pave the way to combining the ratios into a single divisor. First, let's start by multiplying both of the ratios, written in multiplicative form, by unity.

$$a\frac{1}{b}(1) + c(1)\frac{1}{d}$$

Now we will sneakily utilize the divisional property of unity so that both of the divisors are the same. Observe:

$$a\frac{1}{b}\frac{d}{d} + c\frac{b}{b}\frac{1}{d}$$

Notice that this manipulation has not changed the actual value of either term because we are merely multiplying by one! Rewriting the sum in terms of multiplication instead of division and utilizing the commutative property of multiplication from equation 2.4 gives us:

$$ad\frac{1}{b}\frac{1}{d} + cb\frac{1}{b}\frac{1}{d}$$

Now, we simply use equation 2.23 to combine the two divisors into one and we will have:

$$ad\frac{1}{bd} + cb\frac{1}{bd}$$

Notice that the two divisors are now exactly the same, one divided by bd. Since they are the same we can now use the distributive property in reverse to pull out the common ratio. Doing this produces:

$$(ad + bc)\frac{1}{bd}$$

Our final step is to rewrite the statement in terms of division:

$$\frac{ad + bc}{bd}$$

It may have taken a while to get here but the important thing is that we got here. Through this method we can write any sum of division with a single divisor. Formalizing we have:

Equation 5.6

$$\frac{a}{b} + \frac{c}{d} = \frac{ad + bc}{bd}$$

Section 5.5 – Multiplying exponential expressions

Consider that we need to multiply two exponential expressions with coefficients. Mathematically it would look like this:

$$(ax^n)(bx^L)$$

The first thing that can be done is to use the commutative property of multiplication to rearrange the variables.

$$abx^n x^L$$

The first product, ab, is simply a product of two variables, something covered in chapter 2. The second product, the two exponential variables in x, was conquered in chapter 3 and should be no problem. We simply add the exponents.

Equation 5.7

$$(ax^n)(bx^L) = abx^{n+L}$$

Notice that we were only allowed to combine the exponents because we were dealing with the same base variable. If, however, we multiplied two exponential expressions with different base variables we would not be able to add the exponents. Observe:

$$(ax^n)(by^L) = abx^ny^L$$

And we can go no further with this example because our product rule only treated instances of the same base variable.

Section 5.6 – Maintaining Equality:

Often times in mathematics it is necessary to manipulate a given equation to reveal useful information. This manipulation is brought about by applying properly chosen mathematical operations in the correct sequence. Thus this section is meant to address the logic behind applying an operation to an equation while maintaining equality.

Recall that we can only call two variables equal if the stack of representative currency is exactly the same height and type. So let's equate two variables to each other.

$$b = c$$

Although we do not know exactly how much each variable represents, we do know that they occupy the same exact height and type because our equation says so.

First, let's contemplate addition. Recall that addition changes the height of a given stack of currency a prescribed number of units. Thus if we add some number 'n' to b then the height of the left side of the equation would increase by n units . Since the height of b + n no longer coincides with c, the relationship is no longer an equation. We must, in general, replace our equal sign with a not-equal sign.

$$b + n \neq c$$

So the question we are confronted with now is how do we make the two sides equal again? Recall that equality is determined by both sides having the same height of the same currency. Obviously the only sure fire way to do this is to add the same number of 'n' units to c also. This produces:

$$b + n = c + n$$

And we have brought both sides back into convergence and can use the equal sign to designate the relationship between them. Thus, if we add anything to one side of an equation we must add that same amount to the other side of the equation to maintain equality. Of course, the reader will be reminded that subtraction is defined within addition and thus these results are equally applicable towards subtraction with the required assumptions.

Let's now turn our attention towards multiplication. Suppose we again start with a given equation that needs to be manipulated:

$$b = c$$

If we were to multiply the left side by some number 'n' we would lose the identity by the same argument used before; the heights of the currency stacks representing the two sides of the equation would not be the same. To maintain the equality we must again repeat the same manipulation to the right side so that the respective heights are again congruent. Generally this involves multiplying the right side by 'n' also.

$$nb = nc$$

This keeps the validity of the equation and we can continue on our way. So when you multiply one side of the equation you must repeat the multiplication on the other side to maintain equality.

In fact this rule applies to all mathematical operations. If an operation is applied to one side of an equation then that same operation must be applied to the other side. If this tenant is kept then the equation will always remain valid.

Section 5.7 – The Quadratic Formula:

Consider the following quadratic equation in variable x.

Equation 5.8

$$Sx^2 + Tx + U = 0$$

This equation is known to be quadratic in x because there is a direct sequence in the powers of the variable x; 2, 1, then zero. The variable S is known as the quadratic coefficient because it is multiplied by the squared power of the variable x. T is known as the linear coefficient since it is within the linear term, meaning the variable x is raised to the first power. The last term, U, is known as the constant coefficient since it is multiplied by the variable x raised to the zeroith power. These coefficients, S, T, and U, are usually represented by known values, but not necessarily so. The only real restriction to the coefficients is that they do not contain the variable x within their definitions.

The main goal in all mathematics is to find specified values of a given variable that makes an equation true. Since this quadratic equation is determined by the variable x, we must then seek the values of this variable that will cause the left hand side of the equation to be equal to zero and therefore make the equation valid. Finding these specified values of x will require us to derive a very powerful tool known as the quadratic formula.

The derivation for the quadratic formula rests upon the two results obtained for the repeated multiplication of a two termed parenthesis in equation 5.2:

$$(x + b)(x + b) = x^2 + 2bx + b^2$$

And also equation 5.3

$$(x + b)(x + b) = (x + b)^2$$

We can mathematically equate the two results since both of these equations represent different ways of writing a repeated multiplication of a two termed summation:

$$(x + b)^2 = x^2 + 2bx + b^2$$

Which is great, but what's the point? Well first one should immediately recognize that the right hand side of the above equation is in fact quadratic in regards to the variable x. Notice that if we defined S to be 1, T to be 2b and U to be b to the second power then we can write the right hand side as:

$$Sx^2 + Tx + U$$

Clenching our suspicion that it does indeed match the form of a quadratic equation with variable x. Second, if these special circumstances occur in an actual quadratic equation, such as equation 5.8 in the beginning of this section, then we can easily rewrite the equation in the form of squared parenthesis. To illustrate let's again look at equation 5.8

$$Sx^2 + Tx + U = 0$$

With the understanding that S equals 1, T equals 2b, and setting U to b squared.

$$x^2 + 2bx + b^2 = 0$$

If this is true, then we can replace the quadratic with the squared parenthesis:

$$(x + b)^2 = 0$$

At this point we can easily take the second radical of both sides. This will eliminate the second power on the left hand side of the equation.

$$x + b = 0^{\frac{1}{2}}$$

The second radical of zero is still zero. Plugging this information into the previous equation, we can rewrite the right hand side as a standard zero.

$$x + b = 0$$

Now it's a simple task to subtract b from both sides to isolate x on one side of the equation.

$$x + b - b = 0 - b$$

One should remember that subtracting a thing from itself results in zero, thus we can simplify the equation to:

$$x = -b$$

This means that, under our special circumstances, we have found a specified value for x that will cause equation 5.8 to be true and valid. Great! Yet the interest bearing loans that we will be dealing with will hardly ever yield these convenient starting circumstances for the coefficients.

But what if we could, through valid mathematical process, impose these needed requirements on the type of quadratics we will see? What if we could trick the equation, so to speak, into thinking it does contain the necessary coefficients so that the process we just witnessed would fall into place? To this end we will know turn our attention.

When confronted with a daunting mathematical task, it is almost always beneficial to study past victories. Since we did successfully reduce the special case quadratic to a clean and concise answer, perhaps some new insight may be gleaned if we carefully inspect the starting form of this special quadratic.

$$x^2 + 2bx + b^2$$

First and foremost the variable x squared contains a coefficient of 1. But we have already mentioned this before when we set S to 1. If we turn our attention to the coefficients of the last two terms in the quadratic, which we labeled T and U before, we notice that they are 2b and b squared respectively. Although glanced over before, both of these coefficients are based upon the variable b! Thus we could define a relationship between the linear and constant coefficients that would guarantee that the quadratic could be written as a squared two termed parenthesis. To do this we first need to set T as 2b

$$T = 2b$$

We could now divide both sides by 2 giving

$$\frac{T}{2} = b$$

This is important because U is defined as b squared in this special quadratic:

$$U = b^2$$

Substituting the equivalent statement in T we find:

$$U = \left(\frac{T}{2}\right)^2$$

Thus, by using these results just mentioned above we can rewrite the linear and constant coefficients as:

$$x^2 + Tx + \left(\frac{T}{2}\right)^2$$

Now it is important to note that we have not changed anything mathematically. All we have done is state that if we can assume the special circumstances that coincide with a repeated multiplication of a two termed parenthesis then this form of the equation is valid. Thus we can state quite clearly that when T equals 2b, S equals 1, and U is defined as T/2 squared then we still have a special quadratic that can be reduced to a squared two termed parenthesis:

$$x^2 + Tx + \left(\frac{T}{2}\right)^2 = (x + b)^2$$

Or, by substituting the equivalent statement in b as T/2 in the right hand side of the equation;

$$x^2 + Tx + \left(\frac{T}{2}\right)^2 = \left(x + \frac{T}{2}\right)^2$$

Thus we have created a way to find the constant coefficient to construct a special quadratic. Again, great! But we still haven't arrived at a solution for the type of quadratics we will be involved with in later chapters. We need to remove all constraints from our starting quadratic equation for our purposes in interest. So let's approach equation 5.8 again, but for confusions sake let's utilize all new variables that have nothing to do with anything we've spoken about before.

$$Wx^2 + Yx + Z = 0$$

This quadratic equation is quadratic in variable x and contains coefficients W,Y, and Z which do not have any restrictions on them other than not containing an x. Our goal is to use the tools and understandings we have developed so far to trick this quadratic into thinking it is a special quadratic. For instance, the special quadratic equation contained a quadratic coefficient of 1. To accomplish this, let's divide everything by W.

$$\frac{Wx^2}{W} + \frac{Y}{W}x + \frac{Z}{W} = \frac{0}{W}$$

Dividing out the common W in the left most term, and recognizing that zero divided by W is still zero for any finite W not equal to zero:

$$x^2 + \frac{Y}{W}x + \frac{Z}{W} = 0$$

And we have successfully reduced the leading coefficient to 1. Our next step is to recognize that we never stated exactly what the linear coefficient, T, should be. Thus let's just use what the linear coefficient is, Y divided by W.

$$T = \frac{Y}{W}$$

Since our goal is to produce a special quadratic, and since we now have a candidate for T, we can easily calculate the corresponding value of the constant coefficient that coincides with a special quadratic.

$$U = \left(\frac{T}{2}\right)^2 = \left(\frac{\frac{Y}{W}}{2}\right)^2$$

Now, if we recall the results of equation 2.22, we can write the compound division within a single divisor line.

$$U = \left(\frac{Y}{2W}\right)^2$$

Unfortunately, our actual constant coefficient, given by Z/W, does not match the necessary U detailed above. So let's kick it out of the way to make room for this more convenient coefficient. We accomplish this by subtracting Z/W from both sides of the equation.

$$x^2 + \frac{Y}{W}x + \frac{Z}{W} - \frac{Z}{W} = -\frac{Z}{W}$$

The ratio Z/W on the left hand side of the equation can be reduced to zero as a result of equation 1.3. Doing so leaves the equation at:

$$x^2 + \frac{Y}{W}x = -\frac{Z}{W}$$

Now that the meddlesome actual constant coefficient isn't troubling us anymore, we can go ahead and impose the new and purpose built constant coefficient. We do this by adding the equivalent statement for U, under our assumptions, to both sides:

$$x^2 + \frac{Y}{W}x + \left(\frac{Y}{2W}\right)^2 = \left(\frac{Y}{2W}\right)^2 - \frac{Z}{W}$$

We have now created a special quadratic with regards to x on the left hand side of the equation and can easily replace it with the exponential form.

$$\left(x + \frac{Y}{2W}\right)^2 = \left(\frac{Y}{2W}\right)^2 - \frac{Z}{W}$$

Before we go ahead and take the second radical of both sides, we should do a little work on the right hand side. For instance, let's distribute the second power through the parenthesis as in equation 3.3

$$\left(x + \frac{Y}{2W}\right)^2 = \frac{Y^2}{2^2W^2} - \frac{Z}{W}$$

It would also do well for us to combine the two ratios into a single fraction as shown by equation 5.6 encountered earlier in this chapter.

$$\left(x + \frac{Y}{2W}\right)^2 = \frac{Y^2W - 2^2W^2Z}{2^2W^3}$$

Using the distributive property in reverse we may remove one of the common W from the numerator and then divide it out with one of the W in the denominator. This leaves the equation in the following form.

$$\left(x + \frac{Y}{2W}\right)^2 = \frac{Y^2 - 2^2WZ}{2^2W^2}$$

With the right hand side of the equation cleaned up, we can now take the second radical of both sides. This will result in the elimination of the square on the left hand side.

$$x + \frac{Y}{2W} = \left(\frac{Y^2 - 2^2WZ}{2^2W^2}\right)^{\frac{1}{2}}$$

Since we have assumed the radical to be defined within the exponent, we can use equation 3.3 to distribute the radical to both numerator and denominator.

$$x + \frac{Y}{2W} = \frac{[Y^2 - 2^2WZ]^{\frac{1}{2}}}{(2^2W^2)^{\frac{1}{2}}}$$

The denominator of the right hand side could be simplified further, since we could distribute the radical once again. This will reduce the exponential power of both the 2 and the W in the denominator to one and thus eliminate any need for an exponent. Thus our derivation now stands as:

$$x + \frac{Y}{2W} = \frac{[Y^2 - 2^2WZ]^{\frac{1}{2}}}{2W}$$

Finally we isolate x by subtracting Y/2W from both sides. This will reduce the positive Y/2W to zero on the left hand side.

$$x = -\frac{Y}{2W} + \frac{[Y^2 - 2^2WZ]^{\frac{1}{2}}}{2W}$$

Since the right hand side now contains common denominators, we can combine the two under a common ratio as shown by equation 5.5

$$x = \frac{-Y + [Y^2 - 2^2WZ]^{\frac{1}{2}}}{2W}$$

Finally, setting the second power of two equal to 4, we arrive at the formal solution for the variable x.

Equation 5.9

$$x = \frac{-Y + [Y^2 - 4WZ]^{\frac{1}{2}}}{2W}$$

Recall that we didn't limit ourselves in our choice for the coefficients W, Y, and Z. Thus we have found a way to compute the desired roots of any quadratic equation equal to zero that we may encounter during our exploration of interest bearing loans.

Section 5.8 – Numerical Examples:

Example 5.1 – Simplify the following

$$1 - (1 + R)$$

- One should be careful on how they interpret this statement. Notice that we are subtracting the whole of the parenthesis.
- One way to interpret this is to add the negative as shown in equation 1.6

$$1 + [-(1 + R)]$$

- Then using equation 2.7 we can write the bracket as:

$$1 + [-1(1 + R)]$$

- Distributing the negative one gives:

$$1 + [-1 - R]$$

- Combining like terms gives:

$$-R$$

- This example is very important conceptually. It shows the proper way to subtract a parenthetic summation.

Example 5.2 – Solve for x

$$\frac{x}{3} + \frac{2}{3} = 4$$

- Solving for x consists of isolating it on one side of the equal sign.
- One method to accomplish this is to first use equation 5.6 to combine the two ratios into one fraction

$$\frac{x + 2}{3} = 4$$

- Now we can get rid of the denominator by multiplying both sides of the equation by 3 doing so gives

$$(3)\frac{x + 2}{3} = 4(3)$$

- Using equation 2.16 we can separate the denominator from the numerator

$$(x + 2)(3)\frac{1}{3} = 4(3)$$

- Now we can use that same procedure in reverse to move the two threes into the same ratio on the left hand side

$$(x + 2)\frac{3}{3} = 4(3)$$

- This move creates the opportunity to utilize equation 2.13 to reduce the ratio to one. Couple this with the fact that 1 times anything is itself and the right side turns into

$$x + 2 = 4(3)$$

- The right hand side of the equation can be multiplied to 12

$$x + 2 = 12$$

- Now we need to subtract 2 from both sides of the equation so that we can isolate the variable x

$$x + 2 - 2 = 12 - 2$$

- Notice that subtracting the two from the positive two on the right hand side will result in zero. Recall that zero added to anything is itself. Thus we now have

$$x = 12 - 2$$

- Now we only need to subtract two from twelve

$$x = 10$$

- At this point we have isolated x on one side of the equation and a single number on the other side. Thus x is solved for and found to be equal to 10.

Example 5.3 – simplify the following statement

$$\frac{5 + 3^2(4 - 3)}{2(4)} - \frac{3 + 2(4 + 2)}{5}$$

- This example requires us to use the tenets of GLEMA
- The first letter, G, stands for grouping symbols, parenthesis and divisor lines
- Focusing on the parenthesis first we perform the desired operations

$$\frac{5 + 3^2(1)}{2(4)} - \frac{3 + 2(6)}{5}$$

- Notice that it was actually addition that was performed as the very first operation even though it is the last component of GLEMA. Yet because addition was within the parenthesis it was first to go. This does not mean all addition was completed at this iteration because one should recognize that we still have addition in both numerators and in between the two ratios as well.
- The divisor line component of G simply means that we need to approach each portion of the ratio as its own entity until all simplifications are finished.

- The next letter, L, stands for Logarithms. Of which we have none, so we can move to the next letter.
- E stands for exponents, and we do have an exponential statement. Performing that operation yields

$$\frac{5 + 9(1)}{2(4)} - \frac{3 + 2(6)}{5}$$

- M stands for multiplication. We have 3 pairs of multiplication in the statement. Performing these operations yields

$$\frac{5 + 9}{8} - \frac{3 + 12}{5}$$

- Our last letter is A, for addition. Carrying out the addition yields

$$\frac{14}{8} - \frac{15}{5}$$

- Now that both denominators and numerators have been simplified, we only have two operations left, the division of the ratio's and the subtraction of the ratios.
- Thus we embark on another round of GLEMA
- Since division comes before subtraction in GLEMA, we will need to perform the divisions. Using a calculator we find:

$$1.75 - 3$$

- Performing the subtraction gives us the solution to our problem

$$-1.25$$

Example 5.4 – Multiply the following terms

$$2x^5(3x)(2x^2)$$

- Don't be fooled by the fancy variables, this is still a simple multiplication.
- Following the pattern we established while multiplying numbers, let's multiply the first pair and then multiply that result into the third term.
- Carrying out the multiplication, we see that 2 times 3 is 6

$$6x^5x(2x^2)$$

- Using the product rule of exponents we can combine the two variable x into a single exponential statement

$$6x^6(2x^2)$$

- Now that our first multiplication has resulted in a clear and concise answer, we can move on to combining the third term. Multiplying the coefficients produces 12

$$12x^6x^2$$

- Again using the product rule of exponents for the variable x we find:

$$12x^{6+2}$$
- Simplifying the exponent we quickly notice that six plus two is eight

$$12x^8$$
- And we are finished

Example 5.5 – simplify the following expression

$$2x^3 + 3x^4 - y^3$$
- This example cannot be simplified further. It is a trick question. None of these are common terms and therefore cannot be added or subtracted

Example 5.6 – combine the common terms

$$2x - 3p + 4y + 2(p + p - 2x)$$
- Recall that common terms are defined as those that can be written in terms of multiplication.
- Even though we seek to combine common terms, we must still adhere to GLEMA, thus parenthesis first
- Combining the repeated groups of addition inside the parenthesis consists of writing p + p as 2p

$$2x - 3p + 4y + 2(2p - 2x)$$
- Notice that we cannot combine any more terms within the parenthesis because p and x are two separate variables and fail the test of repeated addition.
- The next highest operation in GLEMA is multiplication. Thus multiplying the 2 into the parenthesis gives us:

$$2x - 3p + 4y + 4p - 4x$$
- By use of the commutative property of addition, we can shuffle the order of the terms until all of the x are listed, then the p, then the y

$$2x - 4x - 3p + 4p + 4y$$
- Notice that as we shuffled the terms, the sign directly to the left of a particular term remained with the term. This is important because four units of debt does not become positive when the commutative property is applied.
- Our next task is to combine the like terms. This can be done by utilizing the distributive property in reverse to pull out the common variable from the respective terms.

$$(2 - 4)x + (-3 + 4)p + 4y$$
- Again, it is important to notice that the negative signs stayed with the original number. You must keep track of what is negative and what is positive.
- Performing the addition within the parenthesis gives:

$$-2x + p + 4y$$
- And we have successfully completed this example

Example 5.7 – Simplify the following

$$p(3p - 4xy)$$

- This example merely needs to distribute the p across the parenthesis
- Doing so yields

$$3pp - 4xyp$$

- Combining the two p into an exponential term gives us

$$3p^2 - 4xyp$$

- Notice we cannot combine the two terms through multiplication, nor through any other operation, and it is therefore simplified.

Example 5.8 – Solve for the greatest root of x

$$x^2 + 4x - 3 = 0$$

- Example 5.8 consists of finding the greatest root of the quadratic equation. This added qualifier of 'the greatest root' is to keep the wayward mathematicians from complaining. Pay it no mind, we can simply use the quadratic formula, repeated below for your convenience

$$x = \frac{-Y + [Y^2 - 4WZ]^{\frac{1}{2}}}{2W}$$

- Thus our main concern is properly assigning the coefficients to the equation.
- Recall that our Quadratic coefficient, the one multiplied by x squared, was given as W
- The linear coefficient was defined as Y
- The constant coefficient was Z
- Thus W = 1, Y = 4 and Z = - 3
- It is very important that you understand that Z is equal to a NEGATIVE three and not a positive three. This comes about because we could list the starting equation as:

$$x^2 + 4x + (-3) = 0$$

- And then it is obvious that the linear coefficient is negative three
- Substituting these values into the quadratic formula gives us:

$$x = \frac{-(4) + [(4)^2 - 4(1)(-3)]^{\frac{1}{2}}}{2(1)}$$

- We will again have to utilize the tenets of GLEMA to go forward
- The largest grouping symbol in this case is the divisor line. The second largest will be the bracket in the numerator which can be interpreted as inside the divisor's numerator group
- Thus the bracket deserves our attention at this point.
- Inside the bracket we will again have to apply GLEMA. Since there is no further grouping symbols or Logarithms, we can move to the exponents inside the brackets

$$x = \frac{-(4) + [16 - 4(1)(-3)]^{\frac{1}{2}}}{2(1)}$$

- Now that the exponent is dealt with, we can move to multiplication inside the brackets
- Notice that we will be multiplying a positive four with a negative three and will not be touching the first negative sign in the bracket

$$x = \frac{-(4) + [16 - (-12)]^{\frac{1}{2}}}{2(2)}$$

- We may now move to the last letter in GLEMA for the bracket, A for addition. Subtracting a negative 12 from a positive 16 results in

$$x = \frac{-(4) + [28]^{\frac{1}{2}}}{2(2)}$$

- Now that the bracket has been simplified we can divert our attention to the next largest grouping symbol, the divisor line
- The ratio contains multiplication, a subtraction, and an exponent. Thus we need to tackle the exponent first
- The second radical of 28 can be found most easily through a calculator

$$x = \frac{-(4) + 5.2915\dots}{2(2)}$$

- Easy enough. Next is multiplication. In the numerator we need to multiply the negative symbol with the four, or a negative one with a positive four if you'd like to see it that way.

$$x = \frac{-4 + 5.2915\dots}{2(2)}$$

- And Don't forget to multiply the denominator

$$x = \frac{-4 + 5.2915\dots}{4}$$

- The last part of GLEMA is addition, Performing this operation yields

$$x = \frac{1.2915\dots}{4}$$

- Now we simply divide by four to obtain

$$x = .322\dots$$

- A hard fought battle to be sure.

Chapter 6 – Summation of Arbitrary Strings

Section 6.1 – Sigma Summation

Multiplication, as we have already seen, is a shorthand way of writing recurrent and exact groups of addition. Unfortunately, many operations in interest require large strings of non-repeating addition. Because multiplication fails to write the necessary large strings of addition that govern many of the interest mathematics in a manageable style, we will need to explore the sigma notation.

Sigma summation is another, but more generalized, shorthand for addition. It is powerful because we can drop the exact and repeatable constraint and allow for a larger swath of addition. Below is an example of the sigma summation, or notation, and its corresponding addition.

$$2 + 4 + 6 + 8 = \sum_{L=1}^{4} 2L$$

The large symbol, Σ, is the upper case Greek letter sigma. Underneath the sigma are the index variable L and the lower bound of summation, in this case 1. Atop the sigma is the upper bound of summation, in our example a 4. The lower and upper bound of summation dictate what value L will start and end with. To the right of the sigma sits the formula, the actual meat of the sigma notation.

The sigma summation operates by substituting the lower bound of summation into the formula's index variable. This creates the first term of the sigma summation. The index is then stepped a unit at a time (with each step creating another term) until the upper bound is reached and the summation terminates. Using our sigma summation example above, we will illustrate the process presently.

The lower bound of summation is defined at the bottom of the sigma as one. Thus the first term of the summation is given by substituting the lower bound for L in the formula.

$$2(1) = 2$$

The index then steps one unit to 2. Substituting this new value for L into the formula we will find our second term:

$$2(2) = 4$$

Again the index steps one unit to 3. The formula will now give:

$$2(3) = 6$$

Once more the index steps by a unit to the value of 4. Since a 4 sat on top of the sigma, we know that it is the upper bound of summation and the summation will end with this last term.

$$2(4) = 8$$

All we need to do now is to combine all of the terms into one summation string, starting with L equal to one and ending with L equal to 4, and we'll have expanded the sigma summation.

$$\sum_{L=1}^{4} 2L = 2 + 4 + 6 + 8$$

The last sigma summation was a little boring. To make things a little more interesting, let's consider a more complex sigma summation and its corresponding summation.

$$\sum_{L=1}^{\infty} \frac{z^L}{L!} = \frac{z^1}{1} + \frac{z^2}{2} + \frac{z^3}{6} + \cdots$$

This sigma summation is a definition of the constant e raised to the exponent z. One will recall that the constant e was also introduced in the logarithm chapter as the base for the natural logarithm. Notice that we have changed the bounds for the sigma notation, L now starts at 0 and continues through all of the positive integers to infinity. Obviously it is impossible to write out the entire summation series on the right hand side of the equation because we can't write an infinite amount of terms. The key here though is to realize that we are still able to write the idea of an infinite summation in one nice, neat, and concise sigma notation.

As a side note to the interested student, the exclamation mark indicates a factorial. We will not cover the factorial in this text as it is unnecessary for a basic understanding of interest bearing accounts. But the concept is not hard and I'd encourage any interested student to research it.

Section 6.2 – The constant coefficient:

The sigma summation is no different than any of the other operations we have studied and contains generalized logical properties that we could potentially exploit in future chapters. One such property is the constant coefficient property of summations. The argument goes something like this:

Consider a summation consisting of a constant coefficient multiplied by the index variable. Mathematically it would like this:

$$\sum_{K=1}^{m} cK$$

Where the variable c is some number not associated with the index variable K. Our first step will be to write out the actual summation in long form. Doing this, while aware that our upper bound is m, produces:

$$c(1) + c(2) + \cdots + c(m-1) + c(m)$$

Notice that every term within the summation series contains the variable c. This fact allows us to factor the common c out of each term by the distributive property in reverse.

$$c(1 + 2 + \cdots (m-1) + m)$$

Now the only thing left to do is to recognize that the parenthetic term is still summation and can be written in the form of a sigma notation. Thus we have removed the constant c entirely from the sigma summation.

Equation 6.1

$$\sum_{K=1}^{m} cK = c \sum_{K=1}^{m} K$$

I would like to take the time to head off a potential source of confusion for some readers. The letter c in our equation is called a constant, but it is by definition a variable because it is a letter. This can be explained away by the fact that it is not associated with the index K. Since it isn't connected to K, and does not change when K does, we can treat it as a constant with respect to K. A little confusing to be sure, but hopefully that helped clear up a potential road block.

Section 6.3 – Sum of units:

Consider the following sigma summation:

$$\sum_{T=1}^{D} 1$$

We wonder, since we are dealing with a known value in the formula, if we can't find a simpler way to write this sigma summation. Our first step in this quest is to write out each of the terms that correlate with each of the indices. Since the lower bound starts at one, our first index is T = 1. Plugging this into the formula we find… well wait a moment, there is no T in the formula. The formula simply states the number one and nothing else.

We encountered a similar situation during the last argument in which the variable c was called a constant because it was not associated with K. We could also interpret the formula in this summation to be constant in T and therefore the formula does not change as T does. Thus we could say that when T equals 1 our formula is 1. When T is 2, our formula is still 1. When T is anything, we still get a formula value of 1. If we then wished to write all of the D indexed terms in long form addition we would find:

$$1 + 1 + \cdots + 1$$

Our task now is to simply add all of the ones together. Of course, since adding a number to itself repeatedly is the definition of multiplication, and since we have D total groups of one, we could easily define the statement above as:

$$D(1) = D$$

Meaning D groups of one added together is equal to D, just as equation 2.3 showed us. Thus adding a sigma summation of the formula '1' from a lower bound of 1 to an upper bound of D produces:

Equation 6.2

$$\sum_{T=1}^{D} 1 = D$$

With this understood, let's approach something that may seem counter intuitive at first. What would happen if the lower bound of summation was 0, instead of 1?

$$\sum_{T=0}^{D} 1$$

Before we jump too far into a convoluted argument, let's use what we have already learned. First, at T equals zero our formula will produce a value of 1 because the formula is constant in T. Second, notice that after the first index of T equals zero, our previous sigma notation is fully represented because the index still has to go through all the numbers from 1 to D. Thus, after the lower bound of T equals zero is tallied we would have:

$$\sum_{T=0}^{D} 1 = 1 + \sum_{T=1}^{D} 1$$

Using equation 6.2 above, we can equate the far right sigma as D. Doing this gives:

Equation 6.3

$$\sum_{T=0}^{D} 1 = 1 + D$$

The moral of the argument is to be wary of the bounds of summation as they can affect the final answer.

Section 6.4 – Sum of successive numbers:

Consider the summation of successive numbers and its equivalent sigma representation below

$$\sum_{x=1}^{v} x = 1 + 2 + \cdots + v$$

Since we are again dealing with known values in the formula, we wonder if we can't find a generalized answer for the sigma summation regardless of the upper bound v. This may seem difficult because this summation diverges, meaning as v becomes larger the results become more distant. For instance, an increase in the upper bound v from 3 to 4 only corresponds to a 4 unit gap between the two final summations. But an increase in v from a value of 999 to 1000 causes a thousand unit gap, and it gets worse as we progress further.

Perhaps if we focused on the abstract mathematics we might find a pattern we could use. For instance, let's look closer at the ending values of the summation. Although we do not have an actual value for v, the upper bound of summation, we can still label the final addition as the variable v. This will prove to be an important point because of the next logical question; what number comes before v? The answer to this has already been listed during the buildup to equation 6.1. Hopefully it was such an obvious fact that you didn't even notice. The number that comes before v is the number one less than v, or v minus one; $(v - 1)$. Using this same notation we could list the 2nd number before v as $(v - 2)$. The 3rd as $(v - 3)$, and so on and so on. Expanding our notation a little bit to reflect this new information we could write the summation as:

$$1 + 2 + 3 + \cdots + (v - 3) + (v - 2) + (v - 1) + v$$

One should recall that we don't necessarily have to add these numbers together in the order we are presently given. Under the results of the commutative property of addition, we know that we can mix and match the string of addends into any sequence we want. For the next portion of our argument, let's assume that v is restricted to even numbers, numbers that are wholly divisible by 2. If this assumption is allowed then we can divide the whole of v into two sets of numbers, one half containing the smaller numbers from 1 to v/2 and the other half containing all the rest.

$$1st\ half = 1 + 2 + 3 + \cdots$$
$$2nd\ half = \cdots + (v - 1) + (v - 2) + v$$

Now, let's rearrange the latter half so that we list the string of numbers in decreasing order. Our two halves will now look like:

$$1st\ half = 1 + 2 + 3 + \cdots$$
$$2nd\ half = v + (v - 1) + (v - 2) \cdots$$

What would happen if we were to add the first number from the first half and the first listed number from the second half successively? First we would have

$$1 + v = v + 1$$

Continuing this pattern, the second addition would consist of the second number, 2, and the second number from the latter half, v minus 1;

$$2 + (v - 1) = v + 1$$

Then the third pair would be selected from the next number in each respective line:

$$3 + (v - 2) = v + 1$$

If we continue this pattern then each pair would combine to the value of v + 1. Once each number has been paired up the string of the results added together would be given as:

$$(v + 1) + (v + 1) + (v + 1) + \cdots$$

Notice that we now have repeated groups of addition. The definition of multiplication! The next question is how many groups of (v + 1) are present? Recall that each parenthetic statement (v + 1) was constructed by one number from the first half and one number from the second half. Thus we could deduce that there is a one to one correlation between the number of groups of (v + 1) and the amount of numbers in a single group. Since one of the groups contains exactly half of v, we know that there are v/2 groups of (v + 1) added together. Rewriting the addition in terms of multiplication gives:

$$\frac{v}{2}(v + 1)$$

Thus we have found a short concise answer for the summation of successive numbers, assuming v is even.

Equation 6.4

$$\sum_{x=1}^{v} x = \frac{v(v + 1)}{2}$$

We have done a great job so far, we have proven a concise statement for half of the positive numbers. But that still leaves a large swath of the number tower omitted from our findings. Isn't there a way we could bring the odd numbers into the fold?

First, Recall equation 2.12 from chapter two that defined an odd number as an even number plus one. Thus we could construct an odd number by adding one to our assumed even value of v.

$$q = v + 1 = odd$$

Thus we could easily label the upper bound of an odd successive summation as:

$$\sum_{x=1}^{q} x = \sum_{x=1}^{v+1} x$$

Writing out the sigma summation in long form we will have:

$$1 + 2 + \cdots + v + (v + 1)$$

The key to mathematics is to use what we already know to explore what we have not seen. The fact is we already know the addition of the numbers one to v. It is defined by equation 6.4. To aid in our derivation, let's bracket this term in the summation so we can easily transition to a result.

$$[1 + 2 + \cdots + (v - 1) + v] + (v + 1)$$

Because the bracketed statement is defined by equation 6.4 we can easily insert the concise multiplication statement into the brackets

$$\left[\frac{v}{2}(v + 1)\right] + (v + 1)$$

And viola, we only have two terms of addition to deal with now. But, even better, both terms contain the number (v + 1). Thus we could use the distributive property in reverse to pull out that number.

$$\left[\frac{v}{2}(v + 1)\right] + (v + 1) = (v + 1)\left(\frac{v}{2} + 1\right)$$

Now we can use equation 5.6 to combine the parenthetic statement on the right into a single divisor line:

$$= (v + 1)\left(\frac{v + 2}{2}\right)$$

Again we have found a concise multiplication that defines the summation of successive numbers. The final step is to substitute the variable q into the equation. To do this, let's first recall that:

$$q = v + 1$$

And if we added one to both sides we would find that

$$q + 1 = v + 2$$

Using these two statements above to substitute into our result we now have:

$$(v + 1)\left(\frac{v + 2}{2}\right) = q\left(\frac{q + 1}{2}\right)$$

Therefore we have found that a successive summation with an odd upper bound is equal to:

$$\sum_{x=1}^{q} x = \frac{q(q + 1)}{2}$$

Which is the exact same form we found before! So no matter what the number, odd or even, we can always say that a successive summation is equal to the upper bound divided by two multiplied by the upper bound plus one.

Before we move to the next summation type, there is one other concern that we need to address. Consider the following summation.

$$\sum_{x=0}^{v} x = 0 + 1 + 2 + \cdots + v$$

The only thing that has changed from the previous argument is the lower bound of summation. However, recall from chapter 1 that adding zero to any number doesn't increase the value at all. We could add zero's all day and never increase the value one iota. So for all intents and purposes, we could just get rid of the zero and not affect the total sum of the successive numbers.

Equation 6.5

$$\sum_{x=0}^{v} x = \sum_{x=1}^{v} x = \frac{v(v + 1)}{2}$$

Notice that this result is quite different than the result obtained for addition of units during the last section.

Section 6.5 – Addition of Successive and Unit Summations

One interesting special case that would be worth the time to study is what happens if the prior two summations are contained within a single sigma summation. Consider the following mathematical statement:

$$\sum_{k=0}^{x} n + mk$$

Rewriting this summation in long form, we first allow k to equal zero, then one, then two, and so on and so forth until we hit the upper bound x.

$$(n + m[0]) + (n + m[1]) + (n + m[2]) + \cdots$$

Using the commutative property of addition, we could rearrange this string of addition to list all of the n's together in the beginning and then all of the m's directly after.

$$n + n + n + \cdots + m[0] + m[1] + \cdots$$

Now that we have done this, we could easily reappropriate the long string of additions into two separate sigma summations. The first containing x groups of n, and the second holding the x groups of mk.

$$\sum_{k=0}^{x} n + \sum_{k=0}^{x} mk$$

Thus we have succeeded in separating the addition within the summation into two separate sigmas. Once this is completed we could use the previous results to carry on with whatever we wish to do. Formalizing our results, we have equation 6.6 known as the linearity of summation:

Equation 6.6

$$\sum_{k=0}^{x} n + mk = \sum_{k=0}^{x} n + \sum_{k=0}^{x} mk$$

Section 6.6 – Geometric sum

Consider the following statement known as the geometric summation:

$$\sum_{w=0}^{m} j^w = j^0 + j^1 + \cdots + j^m$$

Our goal is to find a concise mathematical statement that represents this summation. But before we jump into the derivation of the generalized formula we should limit our ambitions to a small known upper bound of summation. This will allow us to deal with a manageable length of terms while still providing the opportunity to glean very important information about the eventual pattern. Choosing 2 for n will serve our purposes nicely.

$$\sum_{w=0}^{2} j^w = j^0 + j^1 + j^2$$

The next step in our derivation is to multiply both sides by $(1 - j)$. This choice may seem random but in hindsight it will seem a palpable choice. Performing the multiplication to both sides will give

$$(1 - j) \sum_{w=0}^{2} j^w = (j^0 + j^1 + j^2)(1 - j)$$

At this point we will focus on the right hand side of the equation and carry out the multiplication as shown in section 5.3. We must distribute the first parenthesis into the second and then repeat. Do not neglect the negative signs while performing the multiplication. Our result takes the form of:

$$j^0 - j^1 + j^1 - j^2 + j^2 - j^3$$

If we now turn our attention to the four middle terms of the resulting product we will find why multiplying by $(1 - j)$ was such a great choice. Notice that the inner terms naturally develop opposing pairs of powered j's. This produces an opportunity to subtract out the common terms leaving only the outer terms:

$$(1 - j) \sum_{w=0}^{2} j^W = j^0 - j^3$$

Recognizing that j raised to the zeroith power is one, we will then divide both sides by $(1 - j)$ to isolate the original geometric summation we started with. This produces:

Equation 6.7

$$\sum_{W=0}^{2} j^W = \frac{(1 - j^3)}{(1 - j)}$$

Which is a nice tidy formula for finding the total of the summation from W equals 0 to 2 given any j not equal to one. This means we can choose any numerical value for j other than 1 (because division by zero is undefined) and this simplification of the summation is valid. Obviously the potential reduction to the amount of work performed is minimal with only three summation terms. Yet, with this understanding of how the geometric summation can be reduced to a single term under our belt, let's expand the summation from 0 to any positive integer m.

$$\sum_{W=0}^{m} j^W = j^0 + j^1 + \cdots + j^m$$

The next step is the same as before, we multiply both sides of the equation with the binomial $(1 - j)$.

$$(1 - j) \sum_{W=0}^{m} j^W = (j^0 + j^1 + \cdots + j^m)(1 - j)$$

Carrying out the multiplication on the right hand side produces:

$$j^0 - j^1 + j^1 - j^2 + \cdots - j^m + j^m - j^{m+1}$$

Once again, the choice of $(1 - j)$ creates opposing pairs of the interior powers of j which can be eliminated by the logic of equation 1.3. After all of the common terms are eliminated we are only left with the two exterior terms. Setting this result equal to the left hand side of the statement:

$$(1 - j) \sum_{W=0}^{m} j^W = j^0 - j^{m+1}$$

The last step is to divide both sides of the equation by $(1 - j)$ and to replace the zerioth power of j with 1.

Equation 6.8

$$\sum_{W=0}^{m} j^W = \frac{(1 - j^{m+1})}{(1 - j)}$$

And we have found a concise approach to summing large geometric sequences. This result will be a great asset to us as we explore the mathematical approach to interest. One should be aware that this formula does not work for j = 1 because that would cause the denominator to go to zero, which is undefined in algebra.

Section 6.7 – Geometric Sum Extended:

Consider the following summation:

$$\sum_{W=0}^{m} j^{WC} = j^{0C} + j^{1C} + \cdots + j^{mC}$$

This summation looks nearly identical to the geometric summation studied in the last section. The only difference being that the exponent C is distributed to each of the addition terms. We wonder, however, if this little inconsistency would cause any notable deviation in the result of the operation we performed before. Well, there is only one sure fire way to find that out: by performing the same operation as before.

To mirror the last argument as well as we can, let's again start with m equal to 2.

$$\sum_{W=0}^{2} j^{WC} = j^{0C} + j^{1C} + j^{2C}$$

Recall that at this point we then multiplied both sides by $(1 - j)$. Doing so produces:

$$(1-j) \sum_{W=0}^{2} j^{WC} = (j^{0C} + j^{1C} + j^{2C})(1-j)$$

Then multiplying across parenthesis by the distributive property again gives us:

$$j^{0C} + j^{1C} + j^{2C} - j^{1+0C} - j^{1+1C} - j^{1+2C}$$

Combining like terms creates… well actually, there are no like terms in this case. 0C is much different than $1 + 0C$, so we can't combine them. And ditto for the other powers of this equation. It would seem that including the exponent C has rendered our geometric series ineffective.

But not so fast, notice that the exponent C is common to all of the terms in the initial summation. Yet we failed to include it in our introduced multiplication of $(1 - j)$. What if we also chose to raise the two terms introduced in the parenthesis to a power of C? Thus our new equation would be:

$$(1^C - j^C) \sum_{W=0}^{2} j^{WC} = (j^{0C} + j^{1C} + j^{2C})(1^C - j^C)$$

And since 1 multiplied by itself any number of time will always be one, we can simplify our statement to:

$$(1 - j^C) \sum_{W=0}^{2} j^{WC} = (j^{0C} + j^{1C} + j^{2C})(1 - j^C)$$

Carrying out the multiplication across the parenthesis of the right hand side with this inclusion in the exponent produces:

$$j^{0C} + j^C + j^{2C} - j^C - j^{2C} - j^{3C}$$

Then combining like terms produces:

$$j^{0C} - j^{3C}$$

Which is a result that matches the form we found while dealing with the original geometric series. This proves that we are on the right track and could conceivably use the same technique for this extended geometric series for any upper bound of summation. So let's go ahead and perform the same operation to the general form first presented at the beginning of the section.

$$(1 - j^C) \sum_{W=0}^{m} j^{WC} = (j^{0C} + j^{1C} + \cdots + j^{mC})(1 - j^C)$$

Then carrying out the parenthetic multiplication on the right hand side we will have:

$$j^{0C} + j^{1C} - j^{1C} + \cdots + j^{mC} - j^{mC} - j^{(m+1)C}$$

Then subtracting all of the common terms out, we will find a similar result to the original geometric series encountered in the last section:

$$j^{0C} - j^{(m+1)C}$$

Equating this new finding to the summation statement yields:

$$(1 - j^C) \sum_{W=0}^{m} j^{WC} = j^{0C} - j^{(m+1)C}$$

Then isolating the sigma summation by dividing both sides by the parenthetic statement we find:

$$\sum_{W=0}^{m} j^{WC} = \frac{j^{0C} - j^{(m+1)C}}{1 - j^C}$$

Finally recognizing that j raised to the zero C is the same as j raised to the zeroith produces the final result for the simplification of the extended geometric series.

Equation 6.9

$$\sum_{W=0}^{m} j^{WC} = \frac{1 - j^{(m+1)C}}{1 - j^C}$$

Numerical examples will not be provided in this chapter because the interest equations only use the sigma summation as a transitionary apparatus. As such we will only utilize the sigma summation on a theoretical basis and may skip the numerical considerations.

This concludes the necessary mathematical prerequisites for a basic understanding of the behavior of interest. The next chapter will begin our actual study of the interest bearing mathematics.

Chapter 7 – The Theory of Simple Interest

Let us imagine a situation in which a borrower approaches a lender with the hope of borrowing money. The lender agrees to loan out a specified amount (known as a principal and symbolized by the variable p) but he wants to be compensated for being deprived of his hard earned money. He therefore offers the loan with the understanding that a rental fee (known as interest and symbolized by the variable i) will be charged after a set amount of time (known as a time period). To streamline the process, the lender will quote the borrower a rental, or interest, rate (represented by the letter r) per dollar borrowed. With an interest rate we can easily increase or decrease the size of the loan without affecting the general mathematics because, as the lender further explains, the interest is actually calculated by multiplying the rental rate with the total amount borrowed at the end of a time period. Thus mathematically we have:

Equation 7.1

$$i = pr$$

The equation above defines the interest fee accrued after a single time period provided we know the specific principal and rate. This will prove to be a valuable piece of information as we progress through the different types of interest.

<u>Section 7.1 – Static Simple Interest</u>

In this section we will focus our attention on static simple interest: Static, because no intermittent payments are made, and simple, because the interest is based solely on the amount of principal outstanding.

To begin our exploration, let's assume a lender offers an amount of money, p, to a borrower with the understanding that if he is not paid back within a specified period of time then he will be charged a rental fee; or interest. The borrower agrees and takes the money to do what he needs to do. Thus the money owed at the time of lending can be written as the amount borrowed, or p:

$$o_0 = p$$

The letter o in the equation stands for the money owed while the subscript denotes how many periods, the agreed upon amount of time, have passed since the money was borrowed. The subscript is zero at this point because the first time period has not passed yet. Thus at time zero, the amount of money owed is simply the amount of money lent; p. If the borrower quickly returns to the lender and repays the principal before the agreed upon amount of time passes then everyone is happy and the story is over.

Well that was a little boring. To spice things up a little bit, let us now hypothetically assume that the borrower does not return the money in time and the period for repayment without a rental fee closes. As the lender warned the borrower, a rental fee in the form of interest is applied to the loan. Thus the total amount of money owed after the first period is the principal as well as the fee for borrowing the principal; interest.

$$o_1 = p + i$$

Or substituting the result from equation 7.1:

$$o_1 = p + pr$$

The interest rate, represented by the symbol r, is often times given as a percentage but can easily be converted to decimal format by dividing by 100. We will be using the decimal format exclusively for our calculations so make sure you are aware of this when you approach a problem in the real world. The reader should notice that the subscript on the variable o has increased to 1 denoting that one time period has passed. If the borrower hypothetically returned to pay off his debt at this point then he would owe not only the principal but also the accumulated interest. Of course the borrower is a man of his word and pays off both the borrowed principal and the agreed upon rental fee and both are happy. Seems easy enough.

But let's now assume that the borrower still could not return the money even after twice the agreed upon amount of time expires. This causes the lender to become upset because he has no idea when the borrower will return. The borrower is also upset because he still cannot come up with the money to repay his debt and risks losing his reputation as an honorable individual. To solve both of their problems, the lender offers to extend the contract by adding another rental fee to the debt. That way he gets twice the amount of money while the borrower gets twice the amount of time. They both agree and another round of interest is applied to the loan. Mathematically this will look like:

$$o_2 = p + pr + pr$$

Or by using the definition of multiplication to simplify the repeated addition we could write the concise mathematical statement of:

$$o_2 = p + 2pr$$

Notice that the subscript has increased and now signifies that two time periods have passed.

Because this contingency plan was so easy to implement, the borrower and lender decide to adopt the practice as a fall back plan for as many of the time periods the borrower should need to be able to repay the loan in full. Thus we could easily extend the life of the loan past another time period by simply adding another rental fee to the total amount owed. For instance, after the third time period passes we would have:

$$o_3 = p + pr + pr + pr = p + 3pr$$

Under the same assumptions, the fourth period passing causes the total amount owed to contain four instances of interest application:

$$o_4 = p + pr + pr + pr + pr$$
$$= p + 4pr$$

At this point we would do well to try and recognize a pattern that we could then logically extrapolate. Luckily a candidate can easily be seen. Notice that as each time period passes another block of interest is added in the form of the product pr. Thus the total amount of repeated interest terms is necessarily dictated by the total amount of time periods that have passed. With this in mind, the general statement for this mathematical phenomenon can be formulated for the hypothetical n time periods.

$$o_n = p + pr + \cdots + pr = p + npr$$

Meaning at the generalized nth time period the borrower would owe the principal amount as well as n installments of the interest fee given by pr. Formalizing we would have:

Equation 7.2

$$o_n = p + npr$$

Equation 7.2 listed above is known as the generalized governing equation for static simple interest. This means that we can specify the exact amount owed provided we are given the variables p, n, and r.

This argument assumed the loan was static, meaning the repayment was made in one lump sum. This type of loan would make sense for small amounts of money but would become overwhelming as larger amounts of money change hands. With large loans the borrower may request, or perhaps the lender will demand, that partial payments of the loan are provided at punctual intervals. Once partial payments are allowed then the loan ceases to be a static loan and turns into a dynamic interest loan instead. So let us now turn our attention to this new field of study, the dynamic simple interest.

Section 7.2 – Dynamic Simple Interest

To begin our study on dynamic simple interest, let us again assume that a borrower approaches a lender with a request for a large loan. The lender mulls it over and then finally agrees under the following conditions. First, the borrower will be charged an interest fee at the passing of each time period. Second, the borrower will check-in each time period and return a portion of the principal to the lender so that he can begin to recover his rather large loan. The borrower agrees to the conditions but insists that since he is returning a portion of the principal each time period then the subsequent interest fee should only be computed with the remaining balance as it wouldn't be fair to be charged interest on what was already returned. The lender agrees to this new condition and the loan is settled.

This new agreement of paying back a portion of the debt and charging interest on outstanding, rather than the entire, principal shouldn't throw too much trouble into our argument because we have been lucky enough to already be using the interest rate. Recall that the interest rate was defined as a rental fee per currency owed. Thus we could easily compute the interest accrued over a time period by multiplying the interest rate, r, by whatever the outstanding principal happened to be.

To begin our mathematical derivation of the generalized governing equation for dynamic simple interest we will again start at time period 0, the moment the loan is granted.

$$o_0 = p$$

Where again, the only money the borrower owes to the lender is the principal of the loan because the first time period has not passed and a rental fee has not been assessed. Two very important things happen once the end of the first time period arrives. First, the interest fee is added to the principal and then second, the partial payment is paid. Just as before, the interest can be stated mathematically as the product of the principal and the interest rate:

$$i_1 = pr$$

We will define the payment to be represented by the variable negative b to reflect that it reduces the money still owed. Thus the total amount of money owed at the end of the first time period will be the principal plus the interest over the first period as well as a payment from the borrower.

$$o_1 = p + i_1 - b$$

Which we can then substitute the equivalent statement for the interest with regards to the principal and get:

$$o_1 = p + pr - b$$

This equation gives us the total money owed after the first time period for dynamic interest. Bear in mind, however, that your interest rate must be given in the same time period metric as your payment period for this to be valid! If the two metrics are dissimilar, for instance an annual interest rate and a monthly payment, then our assumption that both occur simultaneously is not true and our current formulation isn't usable. If possible, the interest rate should be 'massaged' to fit the payment period, but more on that later.

There is nothing wrong with the equation above conceptually, but it looks a little sloppy as far as our future considerations are concerned. Thus with the foresight of someone who has done this before, I will use the commutative property to switch the last two terms to produce:

$$o_1 = p - b + pr$$

The reason for this swapping of order is to track the amount of outstanding principal left over after the payment is made. Assuming the full payment by the borrower goes directly to the original debt, we can clearly say that the amount of outstanding principal leftover is p – b.

Let's now wait for another time period to pass which will result in another application of interest and another payment. As per the agreement, the interest applied at the second time period will be calculated by the product of the interest rate and the total amount of outstanding principal left over. Thus the interest after the second time period can be written mathematically as:

$$i_2 = (p - b)r$$

Thus we can then give the mathematical statement for the amount owed as the total debt, principal and interest, after the first time period plus both the second installment of interest and payment.

$$o_2 = p - b + pr + i_2 - b$$

Combining the common negative b's, by using the definition of multiplication, and substituting the equivalent statement for the second installment of interest will produce

$$o_2 = p - 2b + pr + (p - b)r$$

Notice that the total outstanding principal is now (p – 2b). This will be important once we need to make another interest installment so remember this. Now, one may protest that we could distribute the r into the parenthesis and combine like terms, and that protester would turn out to be correct. However, this way of grouping the terms will gives us a much better understanding of the underlying pattern as we progress forward. Without further ado, we will let another hypothetical period pass causing a third installment of interest and a third partial payment. The third installment of interest will be calculated by multiplying the rate with the amount of unpaid principal. Mathematically this would look like:

$$i_3 = (p - 2b)r$$

Thus we find the total amount owed after the third time period is:

$$o_3 = p - 2b + pr + (p - b)r + (p - 2b)r - b$$

Then again combining the three payments together into a single term we will have

$$o_3 = p - 3b + pr + (p - b)r + (p - 2b)r$$

This equation is beginning to become a little long and unfriendly, so to make this equation wieldier we will attempt to re-write the last few terms using sigma notation. Notice that starting from the right most side of the equation we have r being multiplied by (p – 2b) and directly before that we have r being multiplied with what can be written by (p – 1b). If we got really fancy we could even say that the next product, pr, could be written as r multiplied by (p – 0b). Thus our interest rate r is being multiplied by a summation of rising multiples of b (starting at two and ending at zero) subtracted from the principal. These observations are a recognizable pattern and can be used in conjunction with the sigma notation developed in chapter 6 to produce

$$o_3 = p - 3b + \sum_{k=0}^{2} (p - kb)r$$

Recognizing a suitable pattern for a sigma summation is not something that can be rigidly attributed to rules. It is more of an art than a science and different people can produce different summations out of the same string of addition. If the reader found trouble recognizing the pattern used to construct the sigma summation then there is really nothing you can do other than keep an open mind and a steady eye. Eventually the ability to write summations will become easier.

Notice that our equation for the amount of money owed can be interpreted as containing two spate entities. The first being the amount of outstanding principal left, at this time (p – 3b). The second idea tabulated in the equation above is the sum of the interest installments represented by the sigma summation. Check to see that this equation is indeed equivalent to the previous statement for o subscript three.

As you have just personally tested the equivalence of the statements (you did indeed check that the two statements were equivalent right?) you can verify that we have succeeded in rewriting the same information in a new way. This new concise form could provide us with a gateway to a generalized and concise mathematical statement for a hypothetical n time periods. Of course it will take a little more elbow grease to do this.

Let us now fast forward to the end of the fourth time period. This will result in the application of the rental fee as well as a subtraction of a partial payment. The interest assessed after the fourth time period is the product of the interest rate and the amount of outstanding principal. Taking a glance at the equation for the third time period we see that the outstanding principal is represented by (p – 3b). Thus we have:

$$i_4 = (p - 3b)r$$

Using the equation above and the fact that we will subtract another partial payment we now have enough information to write the equation for the amount of money owed after the fourth time installment.

$$o_4 = p - 3b + \left(\sum_{k=0}^{2} (p - kb)r \right) + (p - 3b)r - b$$

The parenthesis is included around the sigma notation to explicitly indicate where the sigma notation ends. Notice that, even with the sigma notation, the fundamental concepts still remain.

The interest rate is applied to the portion of the principal that is not paid, p – 3b in this case, and a payment is subtracted. We could easily combine the b's together to form.

$$o_4 = p - 4b + \left(\sum_{k=0}^{2} (p - kb)r \right) + (p - 3b)r$$

Focusing now on the last part of the equation, we wonder if we can't include the (p – 3b)r into the sigma notation. Let us start by focusing on the portion of the equation in question:

$$\left(\sum_{k=0}^{2} (p - kb)r \right) + (p - 3b)r$$

Now if we were to write out the sigma notation into its separate groups we would have.

$$\big((p - 0b)r + (p - 1b)r + (p - 2b)r \big) + (p - 3b)r$$

Notice that the last term (p – 3b)r is a consistent continuation of the pattern set up by the first three terms. The multiple of b starts at zero and then increases by 1 until it reaches the end term of 3b. Since this is a recognizable and obvious pattern, we could easily recreate the pattern under a sigma summation:

$$\sum_{k=0}^{3} (p - kb)r$$

This sigma notation has an upper bound of 3 to denote the new included term. With this new sigma summation we can now write the money owed after the fourth period as:

$$o_4 = p - 4b + \sum_{k=0}^{3} (p - kb)r$$

Let's stop for a moment and review what we have found so far. Two main concerns show themselves. First, notice that each time period subtracts another payment from the principal. So given n time periods, n payments will have been made. Thus we can clearly state the principal remaining at the nth time period is given by (p – nb). Second, notice that during the nth time period, the interest is calculated with the principal remaining during the (n – 1)th time period. This interest accumulation will be added to all previous accumulations and will cause an increase in the upper index of the sigma notation by one unit to the maximum index of (n – 1). Combining this knowledge into our model we predict that the total money owed at the nth time period will be given as:

Equation 7.3

$$o_n = p - nb + \sum_{k=0}^{n-1} (p - kb)r$$

$$n < \frac{p}{b} + 1$$

Try this equation out for the time periods we have already computed by plugging in a value for n and expanding the sigma summation. You will see that this equation does indeed describe what we found by derivation.

One may have noticed that below equation 7.3 there is a qualifier for n. this qualifier states that the generalized equation is only valid for n less than the p/b plus one. We will explain this reasoning later. But first let's focus on the sigma summation of equation 7.3. Notice that once n become large, say 200, then we will have 200 terms contained within the summation that must be evaluated. This is an insane amount of work for a single problem. Couple this with the probability of making an honest mistake while performing the operations on each term, and we have a recipe for disaster. But couldn't we use the results of chapter 6 to simplify the sigma summation into a clean a concise statement?

Consider the sigma summation from equation 7.3 given by:

$$\sum_{k=0}^{n-1} (p - kb)r$$

First, let's distribute the constant r into the parenthesis by the distributive property:

$$\sum_{k=0}^{n-1} (pr - kbr)$$

Now using equation 6.6 we can break apart the sigma into a difference of summations.

$$\sum_{k=0}^{n-1} pr - \sum_{k=0}^{n-1} kbr$$

At this point, we can use equation 6.1 to pull out the constant variables, those not dependent upon k, from the summations

$$pr \sum_{k=0}^{n-1} 1 - br \sum_{k=0}^{n-1} k$$

The first summation is exactly the same as equation 6.3 and the second summation is given by the formula derived in equation 6.5. Substituting these into our summation (and mind the bounds of summation) it now takes the form of:

$$pr(1 + n - 1) - br\left(\frac{(n-1)(n-1+1)}{2}\right)$$

To make it a little neater, let's combine the positive and negative ones within the parenthetic statements.

$$prn - br\left(\frac{n(n-1)}{2}\right)$$

Writing the last term in terms of pure division provides our final simplification for the summation.

$$prn - \frac{brn(n-1)}{2}$$

Substituting this new form of the summation into the general formula for simple dynamic interest we find.

Equation 7.4

$$o_n = p - nb + prn - \frac{brn(n-1)}{2}$$
$$n < \frac{p}{b} + 1$$

Our formula is now simplified to a clear and concise statement for any positive integer n, assuming the payment and interest occur on simultaneous time frames. We can now freely turn our attention to the qualifier that n must be less than or equal to the ratio p divided by b plus one.

As mentioned before, the formulation for the money owed at a given time period n can be broken up into two parts. First - the principal still to be paid, and second - the interest accrued. One will recall that simple interest is entirely computed on the amount of outstanding principal. Thus once the total repayment meets, or exceeds, the initial principal amount then the interest charged necessarily goes to zero for the rest of the time periods. Past this point however, our general formula will no longer reflect reality because it will still compute the interest based upon the difference between the principal and the total payments received. This creates an interest calculation upon a negative value resulting in an interest accumulation in favor of the borrower. Even worse, should the borrower become privy to the fact that the computation now causes the interest accumulation to become a net gain, he will simply stop paying and let the interest dwindle down on its own. This cannot stand for the lender as he will be cheated out of all of the interest that should be his by agreement. Thus he must include the qualifier that this mathematical formula is only valid while the interest is accumulating. The question now is how do we mathematically represent the time period when the interest stops accumulating?

To do this we must first recognize that the trouble starts after the outstanding principal is completely paid off. Before this time the outstanding principal is either a positive number or zero and would produce an interest calculation in the regular manner. Thus if we were to restrict the interest calculations to non-negative outstanding principals then we would be assured that our formula is valid. Recalling that the nth time period's interest calculation uses all time periods from 1 to (n – 1), and the fact that if the last time period's outstanding principal was positive then all of the other prior time periods would necessarily be as well, then we would set the qualifier to be:

$$0 < p - (n-1)b$$

Meaning that the outstanding principal in the last time period must be greater than zero. If this is true, then we know that all of the interest calculations will give a true calculation and the equation as a whole qualifies as valid. Solving this inequality for n would determine the point that the outstanding principal becomes negative. Our first step is to add the parenthetic term to both sides:

$$(n-1)b < p$$

Now if we divide both sides by b, (assuming it is positive, we won't go into why we must assume this but you could find the information if you so desired) we can eliminate the b on the left hand side of the inequality.

$$n - 1 < \frac{p}{b}$$

Adding one to both sides will isolate the n and solve the inequality for n.

Equation 7.5

$$n < \frac{p}{b} + 1$$

Which is exactly the qualifier we were looking for. As can be seen, once n is greater than one plus the ratio of p/b our formula will longer be valid because our outstanding principal will no longer be positive.

We will define the critical time period for the dynamic simple interest as the last n that satisfies equation 7.5. It is important to unmistakably understand that the critical time period specifies the last period that interest is accumulated and by extension the period that the outstanding principal is satisfied. After this point, the borrower only owes the total accumulated interest over the course of the loan. Thus substituting the critical time period into the general equation for dynamic simple interest, assuming interest and payments occur on simultaneous time periods, provides:

Equation 7.6

$$o_n = p - nb + prn_c - \frac{brn_c(n_c - 1)}{2}$$

$$n \geq \frac{p}{b} + 1$$

This equation's qualifier is the exact opposite of equation 7.5 because this equation will lock the accumulated interest into a constant maximum that does not change. Any new payments by the borrower will go directly towards eliminating this unchanging interest. Thus given the original principal and the constant payment agreed upon by the two parties we can easily define the critical time period for any given loan. With this critical time period determined we can specify the amount owed by the borrower for any time period before we reach the critical n with equation 7.4 and after we reach the critical n with equation 7.6 above.

Section 7.3 – Special Case for Dynamic Simple Interest:

One special case that is illuminating to study occurs when the ratio p over b equals a whole number, meaning without a decimal. In this instance calculating our critical time period may be confusing for some of the readers. So let's look at it in detail. Using the qualifier from equation 7.5 we find our critical time period to be the last n to satisfy the inequality:

$$n < \frac{p}{b} + 1$$

By our assumption that the ratio p over b is a whole number, the critical time period must be one number less than this whole number plus one. This means that the critical time period must be p/b. To help clarify what is happening, let's specify that the ratio p over b is equal to the whole number m. substituting this into the qualifier gives us:

$$n < m + 1$$

The question now is; what is the greatest whole number that is less than m plus one? Of course it is m! Thus the critical time period is given by m, or the ratio p over b.

Recall that the critical time period determines when the outstanding principal is paid off. As a check that we have indeed determined the correct critical time period we could easily substitute this candidate into n for the part of equation 7.4 that specifies how much outstanding principal is left. At n = p/b we have:

$$p - nb = p - \frac{p}{b}b = p - p\frac{b}{b}$$

Using equation 2.13, we can reduce the ratio to one and therefore the statement goes to zero

$$p - p(1) = 0$$

Therefore we were correct in our calculated critical time period. After this critical point there can be no more interest accumulation and equation 7.4 becomes invalid. Instead we will need to use equation 7.6, the general formula for dynamic simple interest after the critical time period:

$$o_n = p - nb + prn_c - \frac{brn_c(n_c - 1)}{2}$$

$$n \geq \frac{p}{b} + 1$$

But we aren't finished yet. With the further simplification that the critical time period is equal to the ratio p over b, it would be more beneficial to substitute this value into the above equation to find:

Equation 7.7

$$o_n = p - nb + pr\frac{p}{b} - \frac{br\frac{p}{b}\left(\frac{p}{b} - 1\right)}{2}$$

$$n \geq \frac{p}{b} + 1$$

Let's apply a little of our prior findings to clean up this equation into a more pleasing form. First, let's focus on the last two terms of the general equation.

$$pr\frac{p}{b} - \frac{br\frac{p}{b}\left(\frac{p}{b} - 1\right)}{2}$$

Using equation 2.16 twice we can rewrite the two segments as division

$$\frac{prp}{b} - \frac{\frac{pbr}{b}\left(\frac{p}{b} - 1\right)}{2}$$

Now let's use equation 2.13 to divide out the common b's to unity:

$$\frac{prp}{b} - \frac{pr\left(\frac{p}{b} - 1\right)}{2}$$

Our next move will be to distribute the product pr:

$$\frac{prp}{b} - \frac{\frac{ppr}{b} - pr}{2}$$

Next, we can use the definition of exponents to rewrite the repeated multiplication of p into its shorthand form.

$$\frac{p^2r}{b} - \frac{\frac{p^2r}{b} - rp}{2}$$

Now we can use equation 5.6 to combine the two ratios into one divisor line

$$\frac{2p^2r - b\left(\frac{p^2r}{b} - rp\right)}{2b}$$

Using equation 1.6, we can rewrite the numerator as an addition:

$$\frac{2p^2r + \left(-b\left(\frac{p^2r}{b} - rp\right)\right)}{2b}$$

Distributing the negative b

$$\frac{2p^2r + \left(\frac{-bp^2r}{b} - rp(-b)\right)}{2b}$$

Dividing out the common b in the second term of the numerator and recalling that the product of negative rp and negative b will be a positive rpb

$$\frac{2p^2r + (-p^2r) + rpb}{2b}$$

Notice that we now have common terms in the numerator in the form of p raised to the second power times r. Combining these two terms we have:

$$\frac{p^2r + rpb}{2b}$$

Using equation 5.5 in reverse we can write this division into two ratios

$$\frac{p^2r}{2b} + \frac{rpb}{2b}$$

Dividing out the common b in the last fraction gives:

$$\frac{p^2r}{2b} + \frac{rp}{2}$$

Finally we have arrived at a concise and simplified statement for the interest portion of our dynamic simple interest, assuming the ratio p over b is a whole number. Substituting this statement into our general equation after the critical time period we find:

Equation 7.8

$$o_n = p - nb + \frac{p^2 r}{2b} + \frac{pr}{2}$$
$$n \geq \frac{p}{b} + 1$$

Equation 7.8 is the governing equation for the special case scenario of dynamic simple interest.

Although this procedure was long and intense, it is comforting to know that each and every step of the derivation was taken directly from the preceding chapters. Thus if you were able to wrap your head around the basic mathematical principals explored in the previous sections then you will certainly be able to conquer the interest bearing mathematics because it is built upon these concepts.

Section 7.4 – Pre-payment of the Special Case

Since the last agreement worked out so well, the borrower returns to the lender to ask for another loan under the same conditions. The lender agrees and provides the desired principal to the borrower and each go their separate ways. But this time the borrower has a trick up his sleeve. Why, thinks the borrower, can't I pay my check a little early this time, if I do then I will come out ahead! Would you believe this logic? How could the borrower pay less money by paying merely a few hours early? The trick, as we will find out, lies in when the interest is calculated.

To begin, let's assume that at the beginning of the loan the only thing the borrower owes is the principal of the loan.

$$o_0 = p$$

At this point we must recall our new assumption that the borrower returns a portion of the money before the time period ends. Thus directly before the end of the zeroith time period we will have:

$$o_{0end} = p - b$$

Then, once the time period closes the interest will be applied to this new outstanding principal.

$$i_1 = (p - b)r$$

Thus the amount owed at the beginning of time period 1 is given by:

$$o_1 = p - b + (p - b)r$$

If we were to compare this equation to the amount owed after time period one in section 7.2 then we would notice that the term pr is missing from the equation above. Keeping this in mind, let's allow for another hypothetical payment to be processed at the end of the 1st time period, giving:

$$o_{1end} = p - 2b + (p - b)r$$

Notice that I skipped a step and just combined the two payments into a single term of twice b. Due to the timely payment by the borrower the outstanding interest is now given by p – 2b. Thus once the time period ends the interest will be calculated based upon the new outstanding principal.

$$o_2 = p - 2b + (p - b)r + (p - 2b)r$$

Notice that on comparison to the amount owed after the second period in section 7.2 we have again lost the interest term pr. One could surmise that this term is now lost due to our new assumptions of the borrower paying before the interest is accumulated and will never be reconciled. But since no other changes can be seen, the loan will continue in the same mathematical way as before, sans the interest term pr. Any skeptical reader should continue with the derivation and compare the amount owed during any specific time period to satisfy any doubts. Remember there is no penalty in mathematics for doubting a presented finding. A person is really only faulted for being too lazy to verify those findings that are within their ability.

With your doubts allayed we can clearly state that the borrower has shed the interest amount pr from his total repayment by paying just a moment before the interest was accumulated. This may not seem like much, but with an interest rate of 5 percent and a principal of two hundred thousand, this method saves the borrower ten thousand units of currency. A sizeable sum for most of us.

But look at this from the lenders point of view. There were conditions that were agreed upon and from these the lender projected the earnings into the future. Yet this new method of payment by the borrower has made these estimates void because of the borrower being early by one moment, one stinking moment.

What could the lender do to regain his full income?

Section 7.5 – Simple Interest with Frequency.

We last left our lender in a bind because he wanted to maintain the amount of interest accumulated from a loan but can't because the borrower is showing up directly before the moment of calculation and cheating the lender out of a portion of his expected profit. He feels this is mightily unfair because the lender is still assuming the full risk of the loan without the full reward. But what can he do? If the lender were to raise his interest rate so as to recoup his loses then when the borrower wants a new loan he will opt for a competitor who charges a smaller interest cutting the lender out of his potential profits entirely. Going ahead with a full interest calculation even after the borrower pays him would be a breach of contract and the lender would lose credibility and business because no one would trust him. So what should the lender do?

After a little bit of thought the lender decides that he will cut up the interest rate and apply the interest little by little. This process is known as increasing the frequency. The frequency, denoted by the symbol f, partitions the interest rate into equal subgroups that will be applied at agreed upon intervals in between the closing of the time periods. In other words, the interest rate won't be applied in one lump sum, but in small partitioned chunks that when added together will equal the agreed upon interest rate. We can calculate this smaller partitioned rate by dividing the original rate by the frequency:

$$\frac{r}{f}$$

For instance, you may agree to a yearly interest rate with a monthly frequency application. This means that the interest rate will be divided by 12 and each of these partitions will be applied each month. You could also divide the yearly rate by the number of days in a year, hours in a year, minutes in a year, seconds in a year, or whatever else you can associate with time. Also realize that I am only using the annual interest rate as an example. You could set up any time period you wish as the basis of the interest rate.

By increasing the frequency the lender won't lose out on an entire rental fee that should be his by agreement if the borrower shows up a day early to pay. He also won't be in breach of his contract because he is only applying a portion of the interest rate at proportional times of the time period. Now the lender needn't worry when the borrower comes to pay his installment and is effectively shielded from the effects of an early payment.

Thus we embark on producing a model for the static simple interest including frequency. To begin we assume that at the beginning the borrower only owes the principal.

$$o_0 = p$$

We then encounter the first application of the partitioned interest rate. As before, the calculation of the interest is done by multiplying the principal by the interest rate, which in this case is a partitioned rate. To clarify that this is not the first time interval, but the first partitioned interval, we will use a subscript of 1/f

$$o_{\frac{1}{f}} = p + \frac{pr}{f}$$

Another partitioned time period passes and we apply the partitioned interest to the outstanding principal again.

$$o_{\frac{2}{f}} = p + \frac{pr}{f} + \frac{pr}{f}$$

One should immediately note two things. First – the interest accrual is exactly the same as before because, second – the outstanding principal remains the same since a payment has not been made. Thus we have encountered a repeated addition and can invoke the properties of multiplication to rewrite the statement above as:

$$o_{\frac{2}{f}} = p + \frac{2pr}{f}$$

Letting another partitioned period pass we find:

$$o_{\frac{3}{f}} = p + \frac{2pr}{f} + \frac{pr}{f}$$

Here we could again combine the common terms of the interest rate to give:

$$o_{\frac{3}{f}} = p + \frac{3pr}{f}$$

Once again, another partitioned time period passes and yet another segment of the interest is accrued. Mathematically we would have:

$$o_{\frac{4}{f}} = p + \frac{4pr}{f}$$

Let's pause for a moment and look at our results with a keen eye to try to find a pattern we can exploit. One may notice that the number of partitioned time periods that have passed necessarily equals the number of partitioned applications of interest. This observation paves the way to a general formula for a given partitioned time period. Mathematically we could write:

Equation 7.9

$$o_{\frac{L}{f}} = p + \frac{Lpr}{f}$$

We have used an L instead of an n because the partitioned interval is generally different than the nth interval which represents a full time period. Now, since L will continue to increase by a unit value after each partition, it will reach a few special numbers that will be a multiple of f. That is to say that as time progresses L will eventually become a value that will equal 1f, 2f, 3f, or the generalized nf. What then would happen if we were to mathematically encounter one of these special time periods that L is equal to a multiple of f? Let's substitute a general multiple of f for L to find out.

$$o_{\frac{nf}{f}} = p + \frac{nfpr}{f}$$

By reducing the constant terms in the fractions by equation 2.13 we end up with the exact same formula for static simple interest! (and don't forget to simplify the subscript of o with the same method).

$$o_n = p + npr$$

As can be seen by our argument, the frequency of interest accumulation makes no difference in the magnitude of simple interest accumulated over a time period. So the lender can't make any more money by collecting a little bit here and a little bit there rather than calculating the interest accrued right before the payment no matter how long it has been. But that's the key, right BEFORE the payment is added in. If the lender calculates the interest AFTER the payment is deducted then he stands to lose a little money. Thus the lender can use a higher frequency of interest application to recover some of the loss of an early payment.

Section 7.6 – Less-Simple Interest

At this point, the lender feels a little bit better since he was able to counter the brazen attempt by the borrower to rip him off of an interest payment by paying early, but he is still sore. So when the borrower again approaches him for a new loan he decides to pull an ace from his sleeve as well. He will only agree to a loan with the borrower if he agrees to a less-simple interest loan.

A less-simple interest loan is termed less-simple because technically the interest is still only applied to the principal. The difference is that the borrower must first pay off the interest accumulated before the principal can be reduced. So although the interest is only calculated based upon the outstanding principal, a portion of the lenders money is being diverted away from an otherwise potential reduction of principal. This will serve to stretch out the time it takes to pay off a loaned amount, holding the payment variable b constant, and ultimately increase the total amount of interest collected over the life of the loan.

Let's begin with our analysis of the less than simple interest loan. Using the familiar starting point that we only owe the principal at the time the loan is granted:

$$o_0 = p$$

Let's now let a single time period pass. This will, assuming the borrower will pay in equal installments at each time period, result in both an accumulation of interest and a payment by the borrower.

$$o_1 = p + pr - b$$

Let us take a moment to discuss the results for o, subscript 1. We have effectively added the interest amount (pr) to the principal amount (p) then subtracted the payment amount (b). This is exactly the same situation we found for o, subscript 1 in section 7.2. However, we have no idea how much, or even if, the principal is reduced. The culprit stems from the fact that the payment no longer applies exclusively to the principal. It must first cover the interest accumulation, pr, and IF there is anything left of the payment it will then go towards reducing the principal.

Thus we have three possible outcomes we will have to consider in turn. Case 1 - the interest accumulation is more than the payment. Case 2 - the interest accumulation is equal to the payment. Case 3 - the interest accumulation is less than the payment.

Case 1: pr > b
Our assumptions in case one coincides with the following mathematical statements

$$o_1 = p + pr - b$$
$$pr > b$$

Since the interest installment is greater than the payment then the principal will not experience a reduction. Thus the principal remains whole and, when the next time period passes, will be fully applicable towards the interest calculation. Thus o, subscript two, will contain all that was owed before plus a full installment of interest before the borrowers payment is taken into effect:

$$o_2 = p + pr - b + pr - b$$

Combining like terms in the equation above:

$$o_2 = p + 2pr - 2b$$

Since our assumption for this case states that the payment b does not exceed the interest accumulation, pr, then the principal will not be reduced and, again, the full magnitude of p will be used for the interest calculation after the 3rd time period. With this in mind we can construct o, subscript 3.

$$o_3 = p + 3pr - 3b$$

As can clearly be seen, our assumption does not let the payment overcome the interest accrual. Because of this, the principal will never be reduced by one iota. Thus each time period passing will always result in an application of interest with the full original principal intact. This causes the magnitude of each interest calculation to be exactly equal allowing us to use the properties of multiplication to combine all of the interest statements into one term whose coefficient will be specifically determined by the current time period. Following a similar logic, the coefficient of the combined payment term will also be determined by the current time period. These observations allow us to write the general formula for the money owed at the nth time period as:

Equation 7.10

$$o_n = p + npr - nb$$

To highlight our findings, let's factor out the common n from the last two terms by using the distributive property in reverse.

$$o_n = p + n(pr - b)$$

Now since we have already specified that the difference (pr – b) is positive, and since n is also positive, we will have a positive product that will be added to the original principal p! So not only is the borrower paying money without reducing the principal, the total debt is also increasing each pay period! Not a good situation to say the least.

Case 2: pr = b

Case 2 posits that the payment is equal to the interest generated by the principal on the first time period. Thus given the following assumed statements:

$$o_1 = p + pr - b$$
$$pr = b$$

We can easily see that if we substituted the equated statement for b into the statement for o, subscript 1, that we would eliminate the interest leaving the principal untouched.

$$o_1 = p + pr - pr = p$$

One should notice that this is exactly the same amount we started with Thus o, subscript 0, and o, subscript 1, are equal under these assumptions!

$$o_1 = o_0$$

By similar reasoning, the fact that the borrower's payment subtracts out the interest accumulated without touching the principal, we notice that:

$$o_2 = o_1 = o_0$$

And by similar reasoning, so does o, subscript 3. In fact we notice that since the payment never touches the principal, but keeps eliminating the interest accrued, then on the whole nothing changes. The borrower is effectively running in place, never paying off his debt, but never increasing it either. That is as long as the borrower continues to pay his payment on time. Should he become unable to provide an installment payment then obviously his payment, b, will be less than the interest accrued, pr, and case 1 will prevail. But for as long as these assumptions are valid, we can say mathematically that the money owed at any time n is equal to the principal.

Equation 7.11

$$o_n = p$$

Obviously this is a less than ideal situation for the borrower as well.

Case 3: pr < b

Given the following assumptions:

$$o_1 = p + pr - b$$
$$pr < b$$

Then we can say with certainty that the payment installment overcomes the interest accrued and will reduce the principal by an amount dependent upon the magnitude of (pr – b). To help us better recognize a pattern as we progress in our derivation we will first factor out a common p from the first two terms:

$$o_1 = p(1 + r) - b$$

Now since we don't know exactly how much our principal is reduced, we can't say for certain how much to use for the calculation of interest in the second time period. Alas, if we were using numbers instead of variables then we could determine how much was still owed in outstanding principal. But that would be the arithmetic of interest. We seek instead to ponder the algebra of interest, a much more powerful tool.

After a little thought, we notice that o, subscript 1, must be equal to the outstanding principal! We know this because the variable b is larger than the interest product pr and therefore also reduces the principal amount. This means that o, subscript one, must be smaller than o, subscript zero. With this new understanding we can say that whatever o, subscript 1, is, it represents the left over outstanding principal and can be used as a replacement for the outstanding principal for the next time period's interest calculation

$$i_2 = o_1 r$$

We can then state the money owed after the second time period as:

$$o_2 = o_1 + o_1 r - b$$

Then factoring out the common o subscript 1 from the first two terms on the right by the distributive property in reverse we will have:

$$o_2 = o_1(1 + r) - b$$

Now we can substitute the equivalent form of o subscript 1 to find:

$$o_2 = [p(1 + r) - b](1 + r) - b$$

And finally distributing the (1 + r) across the brackets gives us our final form for the amount owed after the second time period:

$$o_2 = p(1 + r)^2 - b(1 + r) - b$$

Since o, subscript 1, was smaller than the original principal then it stands to reason that the interest calculated from o, sub 1, will be a smaller accruement than that calculated with the original principal. Since b is the same magnitude, by our assumptions, then we can say with certainty that a portion of b will overcome the interest installment and reduce the principal further. This will cause o, sub 2, to be smaller than o, sub 1. Thus the magnitude of the outstanding principal is entirely contained within o subscript 2 and we will use that entire statement as the basis of the interest accumulation for the third period.

$$i_3 = o_2 r$$

The mathematical formula for the amount owed at the third time period is then:

$$o_3 = o_2 + o_2 r - b$$

And factoring out the common o, subscript 2, from the first two addends, we find:

$$o_3 = o_2(1 + r) - b$$

Now substituting the equivalent statement for o, subscript 2, we find:

$$o_3 = [p(1 + r)^2 - b(1 + r) - b](1 + r) - b$$

And finally distributing the parenthetic $(1 + r)$ into the brackets:

$$o_3 = p(1 + r)^3 - b(1 + r)^2 - b(1 + r) - b$$

Our formula is becoming a little long for comfort so let's see if we can't do anything to simplify the expression. The last three terms containing the variable b looks to be a great candidate. Focusing on those terms:

$$-b(1 + r)^2 - b(1 + r) - b$$

If we wanted to get real fancy we could interpret the middle parenthesis as possessing an exponent of one and the last term could be written with the same parenthetic statement raised to a zeroth power.

$$-b(1 + r)^2 - b(1 + r)^1 - b(1 + r)^0$$

To help us in our derivation, let's also factor out the common negative b from each of the terms by the distributive property in reverse and then swap the order of the addition. This will result in:

$$-b[(1 + r)^0 + (1 + r)^1 + (1 + r)^2]$$

Notice that everything remains the same within the brackets except for an increase in the exponent value. This presents a fantastic opportunity to utilize the sigma summation

$$-b \sum_{k=0}^{2} (1 + r)^k$$

Plugging this into the equation for o, sub 3 we find:

$$o_3 = p(1 + r)^3 - b \sum_{k=0}^{2} (1 + r)^k$$

Allowing another time period to pass will cause a repeat of the previous occurrences and arguments. I will allow the reader to try their hand at deriving the formula for the money owed after the fourth time period and will simply give the result.

$$o_4 = p(1 + r)^4 - b \sum_{k=0}^{3} (1 + r)^k$$

Hopefully at this point you have recognized a pattern that we could conceivably extrapolate to create the general formula for the amount owed at a given time period. The most obvious thing is that the first term consists of the principal multiplied by a parenthetic statement of $(1 + r)$ raised to a power of the current time period. In the case of o, subscript 4, it is raised to the fourth power while in o, subscript 3, it is raised to the third power. After this comes the sigma notation. Really, the addend inside the sigma summation doesn't change throughout the whole process. It remains $(1 + r)$ raised to the kth power no matter which time period we are talking about. The only thing that changes from one time period to the next is the upper bound of summation which lags the current time period by a unit. Thus we could extrapolate this tendency into the nth time period by labeling the upper bound as (n − 1). Bringing all of this together creates the general formula for the amount owed on a less-simple interest loan during the nth time period.

$$o_n = p(1+r)^n - b \sum_{k=0}^{n-1}(1+r)^k$$

But wait, we aren't finished yet. Immediately, we should recognize the sigma summation as a geometric progression from chapter 6. Using the results from equation 6.8 will simplify our formula to:

$$o_n = p(1+r)^n - b\frac{1-(1+r)^n}{1-(1+r)}$$

Distributing the negative sign into the parenthesis just like in example 5.1 and then combining like terms we find:

$$o_n = p(1+r)^n - b\frac{1-(1+r)^n}{-r}$$

Finally, don't forget to divide out the common negative in the ratio as shown in equation 2.21

Equation 7.12
$$o_n = p(1+r)^n + b\frac{1-(1+r)^n}{r}$$

And we have arrived at the general formula for the less-simple interest loan assuming the payment is greater than the first interest accrual. Notice that there is no qualifier as this equation will give the correct answer for any n until the loan is completely paid off.

Section 7.7 – Numerical Examples:

Note: The numerical examples encountered in the current and upcoming interest chapters are quite involved computationally speaking. As such I suggest utilizing some type of second level calculator device to help you through the intense calculations. Don't see this as cheating, because the understanding of the computation should already have been wrestled with. Now we are dealing with the understanding of the varying governing equations as a whole and it would be a disservice to the reader to become bogged down by the minutiae of the individual procedures. Besides, the breadth of the numerical calculations will invariably suffer from a necessary round-off error. Use of a calculator capable of computing the answer in one fell swoop is advised as this will reduce both human and numerical error. One should be warned, however, that this calculator allowance does not grant one pardon to forget the reasoning behind the calculations!

Example 7.1 – Convert a quoted annual percentage rate of 6 percent into
   a) an equivalent annual decimal rate,
   b) an equivalent monthly frequency decimal rate,
   c) an equivalent weekly frequency decimal rate.

- The interest rate is, not surprisingly, a very important piece of the interest bearing loan. Yet there may be some confusion on the what actual number is used for the variable r in the formulas we've derived
- Recall that it was stated in section 7.1 that interest rates needed to always be applied in decimal formats for our formulas to be valid. This example is then very important!
- The first part asks us to convert an annual percentage rate to an annual decimal rate. Since both rates are in the same time metric we only need to divide the percentage by 100 to find the decimal rate

$$\frac{6}{100} = .06$$

- To reduce the annual rate to a monthly rate, we simply divide by the amount of months in a year, twelve

$$\frac{.06}{12} = .005$$

- To reduce the annual rate to a weekly frequency, we divide by the number of weeks in a year, 52

$$\frac{.06}{52} = .001153\,...$$

- Notice that we don't want to divide the number of weeks in a month because that is a variable amount and hardly ever equal to exactly 4. Of course there really isn't 52 weeks in a year either. The actual total is 52 weeks and 1 day, or 2 depending on the year, but who's counting.

Example 7.2 – What is the total amount owed for a static simple interest loan of 1000 units of currency at a 5 percent interest rate after 4 time periods have passed?

- The governing equation for this example is given by equation 7.2

$$o_n = p + prn$$

- All of the necessary variables are given in the problems introduction. The original loan amount was listed as 1000 units of currency, thus p = 1000
- The interest rate was given as 5 percent interest. Transforming this into a decimal format entails dividing by 100. Thus r is equal to

$$r = \frac{5}{100} = .05$$

- The number of time periods that have passed is quoted as 4, thus n equals 4
- Plugging this information into the equation we get:

$$o_4 = 1200$$

Example 7.3 – Determine the amount still owed on a simple interest loan of 1000 units of currency and a quoted annual interest rate of 5 percent with monthly frequency after 2 years. The borrower pays a monthly installment of 25 units of currency after the interest is accumulated.

- The loan conditions are described above as simple,
- Since we also have an assumed punctual payment of 25 units we can state quite clearly that we are dealing with dynamic simple interest.
- One will recall that the key to dynamic simple interest is the critical time period, n subscript c.
- The calculation for the critical time period is given as the last integer to meet the qualifying standards of:

$$n < \frac{p}{b} + 1$$

- With p equal to 1000 and b equal to 25, n critical is shown to be

$$n = 40$$

- Since our example problem is concerned with 2 years of payment, or 24 months, then our example falls well below the critical time period
- The governing equation for dynamic simple interest before the critical time period is given by equation 7.3

$$o_n = p - nb + prn - \frac{brn(n-1)}{2}$$

- The time period may seem a little confusing, as both annual and monthly reference frames are mentioned in the example problem. But since the interest rate is applied with a monthly frequency, and the payment is also given on a monthly basis, we will call the governing time period monthly, thus n is equal to 24 months
- The interest rate is quoted as 5 percent annual and a monthly frequency. Thus our interest rate is not valid for our calculations. To make it valid we must first transform it into a decimal format by dividing by 100

$$\frac{5}{100} = .05$$

- This calculation shows how much the interest rate is per year, to reduce it to a monthly figure we must further divide it by 12

$$\frac{.05}{12} = .004166\ldots = r$$

- And we have successfully calculated the monthly interest rate in decimal format which is suitable for our reference time period.
- With all of this information under our belt we can now substitute the values for each of the variables and perform the calculations

$$o_{24} = 471.25$$

- Note that if you did not use the exact value for r then you will incur some error in your calculation. It is best to simply leave r equal to (.05/12) and let the calculator do its work. More reason to not solve these problems by hand.

Example 7.4 – How much would still be owed for a loan that is the same as in example 7.3, but with less simple interest rather than pure simple interest.

- Because we are using all of the information from example 7.3 we know that p is 1000, b is 25, r is .05/12 = .004166, and n is 24.
- The governing equation for less simple interest is:

$$o_n = p(1+r)^n + b\frac{1-(1+r)^n}{r}$$

- Plugging in the proper values for each variable and using a calculator to perform the calculation we get:

$$o_{24} = 475.29$$

- This is not much more than was calculated for purely simple interest, so why should either borrower or payer care which is chosen? Well this small discrepancy may not be so small as the values of the variables become larger. Let's increase these values and see what happens in the next two examples

Example7.5 – Compute the amount owed at the end of 10 years for a simple interest loan for one hundred thousand units at .005 monthly decimal interest rate and a monthly payment of 1000 units.

- The critical time period for a simple interest loan with the characteristics listed above is computed from the qualifier

$$n < \frac{p}{b} + 1$$

- Thus the critical time period is 100
- The time period under question is 10 years, or 120 months.
- Since the time period reference is given as a monthly payment and a monthly interest rate, then n must be 120 and is greater than the critical time period.
- Thus the governing equation for the simple interest with the loan after the critical time period is either equation 7.5 or equation 7.8 because p divided by b is an integer and therefore a special case explored in section 7.3
- Let's go ahead and utilize equation 7.5 since we have already calculated the critical time period

$$o_n = p - nb + prn_c - \frac{brn_c(n_c - 1)}{2}$$

- The variable p is given as 100000, r is given as .005, and b is 1000.
- Notice that we did not have to manipulate the variable r since it was already given as a monthly decimal figure and matched the reference payment time period.
- Plugging the values into the variables and performing the calculation gives us an answer of:

$$o_{120} = 1041.67$$

Example 7.6 – Calculated the amount owed for a loan that is exactly similar to example 7.5 but is a less simple interest loan rather than a simple interest loan.

- Since we are dealing with less simple interest, we don't care about the critical time period.
- Less simple interest is governed by equation 7.12

$$o_n = p(1+r)^n + b\frac{1-(1+r)^n}{r}$$

- We have already defined p to be 100000, r to be .005, n to be 120, and b to 1000 in example 7.5.
- Plugging these values into the equation we find:

$$o_{120} = 9418.67$$

- A much larger amount still owed than calculated during the simple interest formulation.
- Thus with the exact same variable values the less simple interest has shown to bring a larger profit for the lender

Chapter 8 – The Theory of Compound interest

Let us imagine that a borrower who is known to keep his word, yet doesn't have the best reputation in the community for being a particularly punctual person, approaches a lender with a request for a loan. The lender is interested in making a loan to the 'bad' borrower as the lender is certain to eventually regain his loan, but he would like some sort of guarantee that the borrower will pay back his loan in a timely manner. After some thought the lender decides that he will take a small gamble with the borrower. But, says the lender, since the borrower can't be trusted to be on time, he will have to agree to a loan that contains an extra punishment for late payments.

One method to persuade a borrower to return the money in a timely manner is known as compound interest. Compound interest is defined as interest that accrues based upon all monies owed, principal or otherwise. This means that a lender assumes that the interest accrued from prior time periods belongs to the lender with as much right as the original principal and therefore subject to the same rental fee compensation. Effectively the borrower must pay interest on interest!

Section 8.1 – Static Compound Interest

To begin our study on compound interest, let's calculate how the total money owed changes with a static loan. Assuming that at the instant the loan is granted the only amount owed to the lender is the principal.

$$O_0 = P$$

We have chosen to use capital letters for compound interest and lower case letters for simple interest to avoid confusion between the two. Assuming that interest is applied to the loan after the first time period, we will have

$$O_1 = P + PR$$

Now, because I've done this before, let's factor out the common P from the right hand side of the equation by using the distributive property in reverse.

$$O_1 = P(1 + R)$$

Allowing another time period to pass creates another installment of interest. Pay attention now because this is where the mathematics of the compound interest gets interesting. As far as the lender is concerned he is owed both the principal and the interest acquired up to this point. Thus the 2nd accruement of interest is calculated with both the original loan AND the interest charged during the last time period. Thus mathematically we can say that the interest r is applied to the whole of the debt from period one.

$$O_2 = O_1 + O_1R$$

Pulling out the common O, subscript 1, produces

$$O_2 = O_1(1 + R)$$

At this point we will replace O_1 with its equivalent statement in P

$$O_2 = [P(1 + R)](1 + R)$$

Notice that we now have two groups of $(1 + R)$ multiplied together. This, we will recall, is repeated multiplication and we can use the exponent shorthand to simplify the statement.

$$O_2 = P(1 + R)^2$$

Again, as far as the lender is concerned, the entirety of O, subscript 2, is his rightful money and therefore it can be applied in the calculation of interest from now on. So another time period passes and we have:

$$O_3 = O_2 + O_2 R$$

Again we can factor the term O, subscript 2, which signifies the amount owed after two time periods, from the right hand side of the equation.

$$O_3 = O_2(1 + R)$$

And again once we place the equivalent statement in P into the statement for O, subscript 2, we find a repeated multiplication of $(1 + R)$. Utilizing the exponential notation again we have

$$O_3 = P(1 + R)^2(1 + R)$$
$$= P(1 + R)^3$$

Let's stop and take a breather and try to observe the pattern as each successive time period passes. Since we are applying the interest rate to the last amount owed, which we will call O, subscript n – 1, to signify the time period before the current, we will always find the amount owed at the current time period to be:

$$O_n = O_{n-1}(1 + R)$$

Therefore, the compound interest simply multiplies the amount owed by $(1 + R)$. Since we multiply a single parenthetic $(1 + R)$ each successive time period then the total number of parenthetic terms must be dictated by the total number of time periods that have passed. Thus, the formula for the amount owed after n time periods is then simply the principal multiplied by $(1 + R)$ n times. Formalizing this statement we find the general formula for static compound interest to be written as:

Equation 8.1

$$O_n = P(1 + R)^n$$

This type of growth is termed exponential, and can grow very quickly should the borrower be late on a repayment. A numerical example will be provided at the end of the section to illustrate how much faster compound interest grows compared to simple interest.

Section 8.2 – Dynamic Compound interest:

Let's assume that the same borrower again approaches the lender for a loan. But this time the borrower asks for a rather large loan and the ability to pay in installments. The lender eyes the borrower for a little bit, well aware of his propensity for being late and unreliable. The lender is interested in the loan, and to the borrower's credit he did pay back the compound loan from the last section. After thinking, the lender agrees to grant the loan but with the stipulation that the interest be compounded so as to persuade the borrower to pay on time. But it's not all bad news for the borrower, the lender explains, because if the borrower were to pay on time then he would be subject to the same deal he gives to his less-simple interest clients.

Why does the lender make this claim? Compound interest is a different beast entirely. How could both less simple interest and compound interest fit the same mold? Well, there is only one way to find out; performing the derivation.

As always, we will begin with the familiar assumption that the borrower only owes the principal at the time of the loan:

$$O_0 = P$$

Since we are again dealing with a dynamic loan, there will be two cyclical issues that must be dealt with, the buildup of interest as well as the punctual payment by the borrower. We will assume that both of these occur on the same cyclical period. Let's also assume that the interest is applied before a payment is processed. Mathematically we would then have:

$$O_1 = P + PR - B$$

Then again, with the foresight of the author, we will factor out a common P from the first two addends by the reverse of the distributive property.

$$O_1 = P(1 + R) - B$$

A few things to notice about this equation should be pointed out before we move on. First, the letters are capital signifying that we are dealing with compound interest. Second, all mathematical values are unknown, meaning we do not know the value of the principal, the interest rate, or even the payment. Furthermore we are not even sure that the size of payment, whatever it may be, is large enough to overcome the first period's accumulated interest.

That last characteristic of our derivation sounds very similar to the situation we encountered in the last chapter when dealing with less-simple interest. How very interesting. Thus we could follow our approach from before and make one of three assumptions; that the payment is smaller, equal to, or larger than the interest for the first time period.

That last paragraph was actually a bit of a quiz on the basic concept of compound interest. Did you pass? The true answer is that, mathematically speaking, we actually don't care whether or not the payment overcomes the accumulated interest and reduces the original principal. The beauty of the compound interest is in the mathematical simplicity of the calculations. Since the compound interest takes all prior debt to be applicable in the interest accumulation, we will simply multiply whatever was owed by the interest rate. Thus the interest accumulation for the second period will be given as:

$$I_2 = O_1 R$$

Adding this to the amount owed during the first time period, and subtracting another punctual payment, gives us the amount owed after the second time period passes

$$O_2 = O_1 + O_1 R - B$$

Notice this was exactly what was done for case 3 of less-simple interest. During that derivation we removed a common O subscript 1 from the first two addends then substituted the equivalent statement in P for O subscript 1. This process seems as good of idea as any other, so let's do it:

$$O_2 = O_1(1 + R) - B$$

Then substituting the equivalent statement in P for O subscript 1 gives:

$$O_2 = [P(1 + R) - B](1 + R) - B$$

Then once again distributing the $(1 + R)$ across the brackets:

$$O_2 = P(1 + R)^2 - B(1 + R) - B$$

Other than the capital letters, this formula is exactly the same as the corresponding time period for case 3 of less-simple interest. Moving forward, let's allow another time period to pass and formulate the amount owed after time period 3. To do this, we will again calculate accumulation of interest based upon the money owed at time period 2

$$I_3 = O_2 R$$

Adding this calculation to the amount owed, and again subtracting another payment, we arrive at the amount owed after time period three.

$$O_3 = O_2 + O_2 R - B$$

Which again exactly mirrors case 3 of less-simple interest covered last chapter. Thus, since the two derivation are mathematically equivalent, we will posit that the nth time period will also follow the same pattern mathematically, although not intuitively.

Equation 8.2

$$O_n = P(1 + R)^n + B\frac{1 - (1 + R)^n}{R}$$

Case 3 of less-simple interest assumed that the interest could only be calculated by the outstanding interest, but dynamic compound interest took no such restriction. Yet, they both share the same general formula. You have just witnessed yet another benefit of using logical algebra rather than numerical arithmetic. We approached two very different conceptual situations and found that they were mathematically identical. Meaning, given the same viable input variables, both situations would behave in the same manner. Such is the power of generalized mathematics. It can simplify seemingly complex situations while unifying conceptually separate conditions into connected results. Thus mathematics merits your study and contemplation as it can, in certain instances, simplify an overwhelming world into a concise understandable whole.

Since we did not have to specify whether the amount owed was actually increasing or reducing at the end of each time period our logical derivation stands regardless of this information. Thus this result completely describes the dynamic compound interest assuming that the payment is provided simultaneously with the interest accumulation. As such, the lender was correct that if the borrower paid on time he would be getting the same deal he gives to the simple interest customers. But, should the borrower be late on a payment he will be hit with a larger penalty of interest than would otherwise be charged if they were dealing with simple interest. It is also necessary to note that although the mathematical formula doesn't care whether the payment is larger than the accumulated interest, the borrower still should because if the payment doesn't satisfy the whole of the interest then the total debt will tend to increase. In the numerical examples we will see this unfortunate circumstance with real numbers.

Because the potential penalty for late payment is much more profitable, and also in the interest of fairness of course, the lender decides to apply this type of loan to all of his clients so that everyone will have incentive to pay on time giving him a secure form of investment with protection against abuse.

But, now that the lender uses the compound interest with all of his clients, even those that are extremely punctual, there will again be the attempt by the borrower to reduce his total debt by paying before the interest is accrued. Naturally, the lender will counter this move by increasing the frequency. Unfortunately, this attempt by the borrower to find a relatively small reduction in debt opened a Pandora's Box in the compound interest world. Let's explore why.

Section 8.3 – Static Compound interest with frequency
Recall that the frequency, represented by the variable F, is a way to incrementally apply the interest rate by dividing the interest rate into a set number of segmented parts.

$$\frac{R}{F}$$

Which is then applied at a shortened time frame a total of F times within the original time period that R would have been originally been applied. Including this technique in the derivation of the static compound interest formulation produces a very interesting phenomenon. So let's turn our attention to this goal. Beginning with the familiar statement that a borrower only owes the principal at the original time of the loan we will have:

$$O_{\frac{0}{F}} = P$$

Notice that we have mirrored the notation of the subscript used in the frequency section of the last chapter but with capital letters. Now, since there is no payment towards the principal during a static loan we only have to take into account the accumulation of interest at the end of the first partitioned period. Since compound interest takes the entire debt to be valid for calculating interest then we will have:

$$I_{\frac{1}{F}} = O_{\frac{0}{F}}\frac{R}{F}$$

Thus the amount owed after the first partitioned time period will be whatever was owed during the last period plus an interest accumulation.

$$O_{\frac{1}{F}} = O_{\frac{0}{F}} + O_{\frac{0}{F}}\frac{R}{F}$$

Then pulling out the common O, subscript 0/F, we would have:

$$O_{\frac{1}{F}} = O_{\frac{0}{F}}\left(1 + \frac{R}{F}\right)$$

Substituting the equated statement for the zeroith iteration of the owed statement

$$O_{\frac{1}{F}} = P\left(1 + \frac{R}{F}\right)$$

Allowing another segmented time period to pass introduces a new interest term based upon the entire amount owed during the last partitioned time period.

$$O_{\frac{2}{F}} = O_{\frac{1}{F}} + O_{\frac{1}{F}}\frac{R}{F} = O_{\frac{1}{F}}\left(1 + \frac{R}{F}\right)$$

And then replacing the amount owed last period with its equated statement we find:

$$O_{\frac{2}{F}} = P\left(1 + \frac{R}{F}\right)\left(1 + \frac{R}{F}\right) = P\left(1 + \frac{R}{F}\right)^2$$

Letting another time period pass produces another application of interest. Thus following our established pattern our third partition would be written mathematically as:

$$O_{\frac{3}{F}} = O_{\frac{2}{F}} + O_{\frac{2}{F}}\frac{R}{F}$$

Removing the constant factor by the distributive property in reverse:

$$O_{\frac{3}{F}} = O_{\frac{2}{F}}\left(1 + \frac{R}{F}\right)$$

Then once again substituting the equivalent statement in P:

$$O_{\frac{3}{F}} = P\left(1 + \frac{R}{F}\right)^2\left(1 + \frac{R}{F}\right)$$

Finally combining the parenthetic statements by the tenants of exponents we find our final simplified formula for the third partitioned period.

$$O_{\frac{3}{F}} = P\left(1 + \frac{R}{F}\right)^3$$

Reviewing the varying formulas for the money owed in each sectioned time period, we notice that the formula follows a set form of the principal multiplied by an exponential representation of the parenthetic statement. Since each partitioned period that passes causes another parenthetic multiplication, we can clearly state that the exponent will be directly determined by whatever the current period is. Thus we could easily extrapolate this form to the hypothetical Uth segmented time frame with little difficulty.

Equation 8.3

$$O_{\frac{U}{F}} = P\left(1 + \frac{R}{F}\right)^U$$

This equation gives the general formulation for the Uth partitioned time period of a given frequency F. With this information we could easily determine the amount owed at a desired partition U if we are provided a particular principal loaned to a borrower at a specified interest rate and frequency. Recall that when we dealt with simple interest we found that frequency did not affect the total money owed over a full time period because when we combined all of the partitions together they added up to the original total. So does compound interest frequency also predict no change in the amount owed?

Recall that in the last chapter we attacked the question of frequency by positing that at some point the number of partitions that have passed will equal some multiple of the frequency. At this point, we could say that the partitioned time period is equal to some number n multiplied by the frequency:

$$U = nF$$

During these special partitioned time periods when this requirement is true our general equation for static compound interest with frequency would be given as:

$$O_{\frac{nF}{F}} = P\left(1 + \frac{R}{F}\right)^{nF}$$

All that has been done is substitute nF for U in equation 8.3. The critical point to this special choice of time period rests in the subscript of O. Notice that we could divide out the common F from the numerator and denominator. This will leave us with:

Equation 8.4

$$O_n = P\left(1 + \frac{R}{F}\right)^{nF}$$

Comparing this with equation 8.1 we see that we have introduced the variable F into the exponent and into the denominator of the parenthesis. So we must ask ourselves; does the F in the denominator and/or the F in the exponent cause our equation to increase in value?

Evaluating whether or not equation 8.4 increases with respect to F is beyond the scope of this book. Any interested student only needs to use the derivative test with respect to F, but this method will not be covered. Instead I will simply supply the short answer to this question and point any curious student to a calculus text.

It turns out that frequency does indeed increase the amount owed over a given time period which is great news for the lender! He can now collect more money during the same time period and the same interest rate. But there is a catch, each increase in F results in a convergent diminishing return. This means that the amount owed will always increase with a greater number of partitions, but it will only increase by a smaller and smaller amount. But who cares, says the lender, if each subsequent increase in F will amass a smaller gain. More money is still more money.

Thus the lender now wishes to maximize the amount of money he can charge on a given interest rate. But how will he calculate what this maximum money owed is? I'm glad you asked.

Section 8.4 –Continuous Compounding

The result of the last section argued that an increase in frequency results in a greater amount of interest accrued over a time period. This prompted an effort by the lender to exploit this mathematical anomaly and find the maximum amount of accrued interest that could be collected over a given time period. Thus this section is concerned with maximizing the effect of frequency on compounding interest.

We might begin our quest by simply inserting the largest number into the variable F in equation 8.4. But one should recall from chapter one that there is no actual largest number atop the number tower. Instead we listed infinity as an idea that represented the value that was bigger than all numbers. Theoretically substituting this into our general equation produces:

$$O_n = P\left(1 + \frac{R}{\infty}\right)^{n\infty}$$

A crafty borrower could convincingly show logically that this new formulation causes the amount owed to eternally be equal to the principal no matter what the value of n may be. This is accomplished by showing that dividing a finite number by infinity is zero, which is true.

Substituting this into our equation we notice that the ratio within the parenthesis will reduce to zero.

$$O_n = P(1 + 0)^{n\infty}$$

Once this step is completed he then only needs to show that 1 multiplied by itself any number of times will always be equal to 1. Thus we now have:

$$O_n = P(1) = P$$

In other words, this formulation completely voids any and all interest accumulation. How interesting that in the lender's quest to maximize his profits he has instead stumbled upon a complete cancellation of interest. So does this mean that we were incorrect in our initial understanding of the effect of frequency? The short answer is no, it doesn't. The problem stems from the fact that our calculation was carried out with an understanding that the frequency would be finite in nature. Whenever we jump from the finite to the infinite our calculations begin to do funny things. As often the case in mathematics, the key to success is how you apply the necessary information.

Instead of just jumping to infinity and plugging it into the equation, let's grow towards infinity. What this means is we want to maintain the value of the frequency within the realm of finite numbers while allowing it to become so large that it is, for all intents and purposes, indiscernible from infinity. This process is known as taking the limit. Mathematically this concept can be written as:

$$O_{nmax} = P \lim_{F \to \infty} \left(1 + \frac{R}{F}\right)^{nF}$$

Where the 'lim' portion stands for the limit as F approaches infinity. Theoretically we have argued that at this limit of infinity (meaning when a number becomes so large it is nearly identical to infinity) we will calculate our maximum amount owed at a given time period n. This may sound like a great stride in our quest, but really we haven't done anything. What number is large enough to be 'nearly' infinity? It turns out that all finite numbers on the number tower are equidistant from infinity. In other words, infinity is so large that it theoretically dwarfs any number we could humanly fathom. So again we have hit a logical wall.

      To move forward in our derivation, it's necessary to state a mathematical property of the Euler constant that smarter men than I figured out.

      Equation 8.5

$$\lim_{F \to \infty} \left(1 + \frac{R}{F}\right)^{F} = e^R$$

Although we won't derive why this statement is true, as the method goes beyond the scope of this text, a curious reader could easily choose a value for R and then apply successively larger values of F to check that the two sides of the equation will begin to merge in value. In fact, an illustration of this process is given in the numerical example section. Any curious reader on how this statement could be logically proven will be pointed towards complex mathematics. As for this text, we will simply recognize that this property exists and try to apply it to our current equation.

Obviously, the introduced definition contains some interesting similarities with the current state of our maximum interest accumulation formula. But there are some differences that need to be addressed. Rewriting our current formulation below for your convenience:

$$O_{nmax} = P \lim_{F \to \infty} \left(1 + \frac{R}{F}\right)^{nF}$$

And then using equation 3.3, we can isolate the exponent of the parenthetic statement to be raised to a single variable F. Doing this gives:

$$O_{nmax} = P \lim_{F \to \infty} \left[\left(1 + \frac{R}{F}\right)^{F}\right]^{n}$$

Now we can directly see the definition correlating to Euler's constant that was introduced above. Thus using the equivalent statement in terms of e we would have:

$$P(e^R)^n$$

Then using the logic of exponents developed in equation 3.3 we can combine the two exponents giving our general formula for an infinite frequency:

Equation 8.6

$$O_{nmax} = Pe^{Rn}$$

As argued through the course of this section, this formula gives the maximum amount of interest accumulation that can be procured by manipulating the frequency.

Below is a figure to help us visualize conceptually how the three static interests compare with each other. This figure was created by taking the same parameters for the original principal, interest rate and period length.

<u>Figure 8.1: Illustration of the Different Interest Types</u>

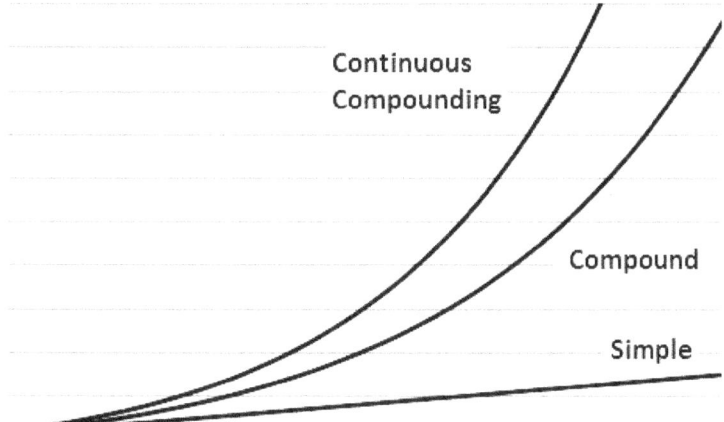

Figure 8.1 maps the amount owed per given time period. The axes have been left blank since we aren't interested in the actual values but the general behavior of the three modes of interest accrual. Notice that simple interest plots a very shallow line and is always below the other two. Continuous compounding, as mentioned above, represents the maximum amount of interest that can be collected holding all other variables constant. Thus it naturally towers above

the compounding and simple modes of interest. Hopefully this has helped you visualize the interaction between the three static interests.

Section 8.5 – Dynamic compound interest with frequency:

This will be the last section devoted to deriving a general formula within the interest mathematics. Unfortunately, this section will also be the most complicated. Even more unfortunate, nearly all real world loans fall under this category. Thus understanding of this section is critical if the reader desires a real world understanding of the interest. With this warning in place, let's begin the last derivation section.

Let's assume that one day our familiar lender is approached by a prospective borrower that wishes for a large sum of money in the form of a loan. We don't necessarily care how large the loan is, but let's imagine that it is large enough to warrant the borrower the desire to pay back the loan with relatively small but constant and punctual payments over time. The lender, partially because he wishes to protect from the effects of an early payment and partially because he could squeeze a larger profit by utilizing the concept of frequency, agrees to the loan provided that he may compound the interest with a given frequency. The borrower agrees to the terms because he needs the money bad enough and the loan is settled.

With the particulars of the loan settled, we can now proceed with the mathematical behavior of a dynamic compound interest loan with frequency. We begin our derivation by starting with the familiar assumption that at the time of the loan the borrower owes only the principal.

$$O_{\frac{0}{F}} = P$$

Notice that the subscript has been written as a ratio to allow for the frequency to readily be taken into account. Since we are again dealing with a dynamic loan, there will be two cyclical issues that must be dealt with; the buildup of interest as well as the punctual payment by the borrower. Often the interest rate will be quoted at a larger time period than the expected payment. If this occurs, we will quote the payment period as the reference time period and will then need to 'massage' the interest rate to mathematically match this reference time period. To help the reader understand, this is discussed with concrete examples in the numerical example section.

If we now allow the first partitioned time period to pass then we will need to compute the interest accumulation over this partial time period. Since this is a compound interest scenario with frequency, the interest is computed by the same method we used in section 8.3 by taking the product of the partitioned interest rate and the total amount owed during the last time period. In this case, the total amount owed is given by O subscript 0/F.

$$I_{\frac{1}{F}} = O_{\frac{0}{F}} \frac{R}{F}$$

Now keep in mind that for the frequency to have any effect as a guard against punctual payment it must occur before a payment is collected. Thus until otherwise stated we will assume no payment by the borrower so that our frequency assumption is appropriate. Conforming to our familiar argument of interest calculation, the new total amount owed after the first portioned time period is the amount owed from the last period plus the accumulated interest.

$$O_{\frac{1}{F}} = O_{\frac{0}{F}} + I_{\frac{1}{F}}$$

Substituting the equivalent statement for I, subscript 1/F,

$$O_{\frac{1}{F}} = O_{\frac{0}{F}} + O_{\frac{0}{F}}\frac{R}{F}$$

Now we could apply the distributive property in reverse to produce:

$$O_{\frac{1}{F}} = O_{\frac{0}{F}}\left(1 + \frac{R}{F}\right)$$

Directly substituting the equated statement for the amount owed during the zeroith partitioned time period gives:

$$O_{\frac{1}{F}} = P\left(1 + \frac{R}{F}\right)$$

Our result states the amount owed after the first partitioned time period passes in terms of our agreed upon quantities P, R, and F. Of course the equation above is only the first of a great many steps that we need to complete so let's allow for another partitioned time period to pass. This creates another application of the partial interest formulated in the same manner as before:

$$I_{\frac{2}{F}} = O_{\frac{1}{F}}\frac{R}{F}$$

This is then added to whatever amount was owed during the last period giving us our first formulation for the amount owed after the 2nd portioned time period.

$$O_{\frac{2}{F}} = O_{\frac{1}{F}} + I_{\frac{2}{F}}$$

We can then substitute the equivalent statement for I, subscript 2/F, and then quickly remove the common factor from the resulting terms in the same manner as before.

$$O_{\frac{2}{F}} = O_{\frac{1}{F}}\left(1 + \frac{R}{F}\right)$$

Substituting the equivalent statement for O, subscript 1/F, into the above statement gives the amount owed at partial time period 2:

$$O_{\frac{2}{F}} = P\left(1 + \frac{R}{F}\right)\left(1 + \frac{R}{F}\right)$$

And of course simplifying the statement by utilizing the definition of exponents we would have:

$$O_{\frac{2}{F}} = P\left(1 + \frac{R}{F}\right)^2$$

Let's allow one more partitioned time period to pass for the sake of understanding the method. The passing of a period will create another installment of interest calculated as:

$$I_{\frac{3}{F}} = O_{\frac{2}{F}}\frac{R}{F}$$

Thus the formulation for the money owed at the third partitioned time period would be given by the amount owed in period 2/F added to the interest given above:

$$O_3\over F} = O_{2\over F} + I_{3\over F}$$

Then following the same substitutions as before, first for I, subscript 3/F, and then for O, subscript 2/F, we will arrive at the expression for the amount owed after three time periods

$$O_{3\over F} = P\left(1+\frac{R}{F}\right)^2\left(1+\frac{R}{F}\right)$$

Of course, it would be beneficial if we simplified the expression by combining the parenthetic statements into a single exponential term

$$O_{3\over F} = P\left(1+\frac{R}{F}\right)^3$$

At this point, one may notice that our simplified equations for the total amount owed at each partitioned time period exactly matches the pattern set while exploring static compound interest with frequency. This is no accident because careful examination of the driving forces reveals that under our assumptions we are specifically dealing with compound interest without payment at this point. Thus we can simply use the results from equation 8.3 to list that the amount of money owed at the arbitrary Uth time period (before a payment is made) is given as:

$$O_{U\over F} = P\left(1+\frac{R}{F}\right)^U$$

This equation describes the behavior of the loan for all partitioned time periods before a payment is made. But this section is titled dynamic compound interest with frequency, key word dynamic. We must, daunting as it may seem, account for payments to satisfy the requirements that this lengthy title demands. To do this let's first assume that at some special ratioed time period, let's call it the C/Fth time period, a payment is submitted by the borrower directly after the final application of interest is calculated. Thus if we were to mathematically represent the total amount of money owed at this time period we would simply subtract a payment from the total accumulated debt, given by equation 8.3 above, since the loan was granted.

$$O_{C\over F} = P\left(1+\frac{R}{F}\right)^C - B$$

Now the next step to our derivation is a little tricky so pay attention. Under our assumptions the interest is compounded at a faster rate than the payments can be made by the borrower. This means that before the next payment is processed we must muscle through another swath of interest accumulations. To start, let's focus on the effects of a single accumulation of interest and then hopefully use the results to help us on our way. Fortunately however, the method of interest calculation maintains the same form as before. We simply multiply the appropriate portion of the interest rate by the total amount owed during the prior time period. Thus the interest accumulated at the very next partitioned time period after the C/Fth time period is given by:

$$I_{C+1\over F} = O_{C\over F}\frac{R}{F}$$

Now we merely need to list the total amount owed directly after the first partitioned time period passes. Since no payment will be processed at this partitioned time period, we can simply state that the amount owed is calculated by adding the accumulated interest to the amount owed in the prior time period.

$$O_{\frac{C+1}{F}} = O_{\frac{C}{F}} + I_{\frac{C+1}{F}}$$

Using our equivalent statement for I, subscript C+1/F, we will have:

$$O_{\frac{C+1}{F}} = O_{\frac{C}{F}} + O_{\frac{C}{F}}\frac{R}{F}$$

Then pulling out the common factor from the right hand side of the equation gives

$$O_{\frac{C+1}{F}} = O_{\frac{C}{F}}\left(1 + \frac{R}{F}\right)$$

Now we simply substitute the equated statement for the amount owed at time period C/F and we find:

$$O_{\frac{C+1}{F}} = \left(P\left(1 + \frac{R}{F}\right)^{C} - B\right)\left(1 + \frac{R}{F}\right)$$

But we aren't finished yet. We could, nay should, also distribute the (1 + R/F) into the left most parenthesis. The reason for this will become apparent once the operation is completed. Doing this, and not forgetting the definition of exponents, we find:

$$O_{\frac{C+1}{F}} = P\left(1 + \frac{R}{F}\right)^{C+1} - B\left(1 + \frac{R}{F}\right)^{1}$$

This result provides us with a great opportunity to observe the effects of a compounded interest accumulation. If we were to first focus on the term containing the original principal P we will notice that the formulation of this term has marched unscathed through the payment time period. There is not one iota of difference between equation 8.3 and the principal portion of the equation above. The reasoning behind this phenomenon stems from the fact that the payment is subtracted from the resulting accumulation of interest on the principal and not the actual principal itself. Thus we can clearly state that the form will always remain the same, P multiplied by a parenthetic (1 + R/F) raised to a power of whatever partitioned time period we happen to be in. The other part of the equation, the right most term containing the payment, has also gathered a parenthetic multiple of (1 + R/F). Should another partitioned time period pass it would stand to believable reason that it would simply collect another parenthetic product which would increase the exponent by one. Try it out if you don't believe me, in fact try it out even if you do believe me. Let's calculate another application of interest and apply it to the amount owed as we have done before.

$$I_{\frac{C+2}{F}} = O_{\frac{C+1}{F}}\frac{R}{F}$$

Then adding this to what was owed previous:

$$O_{\frac{C+2}{F}} = O_{\frac{C+1}{F}} + O_{\frac{C+1}{F}}\frac{R}{F}$$

Pulling out the common variable O on the right hand side

$$O_{\frac{C+2}{F}} = O_{\frac{C+1}{F}}\left(1 + \frac{R}{F}\right)$$

Then substituting the value of the variable O, subscript C plus one over F, we find:

$$O_{\frac{C+2}{F}} = P\left(1 + \frac{R}{F}\right)^{C+2} - B\left(1 + \frac{R}{F}\right)^{2}$$

With these two observations confirmed, we could easily say that if some U/F time periods should pass, without encountering another payment of course, then we would mathematically write the total amount of money owed as:

$$O_{\frac{C+U}{F}} = P\left(1 + \frac{R}{F}\right)^{C+U} - B\left(1 + \frac{R}{F}\right)^{U}$$

Again, since we are dealing with specified frequencies and payment plans, after some amount of partitioned time periods pass we will arrive at another special time period in which another payment will need to be accounted for. This will occur once U is equal to C, just like last time. So let's call this new special time period 2C/F since it is the second occurrence of the punctual payment agreement agreed upon by the lender and borrower. Now because the second payment is deducted after the interest accumulation, our first goal in determining the total amount owed after the second payment should be to accurately deduce the total amount of interest accumulated at time period 2C/F. This can be done quite easily by substituting U with another C in the equation above.

$$O_{\frac{2C}{F}}^{*} = P\left(1 + \frac{R}{F}\right)^{2C} - B\left(1 + \frac{R}{F}\right)^{C}$$

An asterisk has been used on the left hand side of the equation to denote the fact that we have not completely finished with the formula for the amount owed at the current time period. Recall that all we have done at this point is to write out the total amount of money owed BEFORE the second payment is processed. Thus to complete the true formula for the amount owed, we need only subtract another payment from the right hand side of the equation.

$$O_{\frac{2C}{F}} = P\left(1 + \frac{R}{F}\right)^{2C} - B\left(1 + \frac{R}{F}\right)^{C} - B$$

Let's quickly dive into the next passing partitioned period which would create yet another instance of compound interest. Using our well known formulation for the amount owed at the time period directly after (2C/F) we will find:

$$O_{\frac{2C+1}{F}} = O_{\frac{2C}{F}} + I_{\frac{2C+1}{F}}$$

Where of course, the interest is defined as:

$$I_{\frac{2C+1}{F}} = O_{\frac{2C}{F}}\frac{R}{F}$$

The reasoning for this won't be explained as it should already be understood. Substituting this calculation for the interest in the previous equation, and then factoring out the common variable, gives:

$$O_{\frac{2C+1}{F}} = O_{\frac{2C}{F}}\left(1 + \frac{R}{F}\right)$$

This result clearly indicates that, just as we encountered before when approaching the 2C/F time period, each passing partitioned period before the 3rd payment will cause another parenthetic statement to be multiplied by the amount owed in the prior time period. Since the amount owed during the prior time period can necessarily be traced back to O, subscript 2C/F, then we are incidentally multiplying that statement by repeated groups of (1 + R/F) after each successive partition passes. This is exactly the definition of exponents given in chapter 3. To prove this mathematically, we will simply allow another partition to pass prompting the amount owed to be given by:

$$O_{\frac{2C+2}{F}} = O_{\frac{2C+1}{F}}\left(1 + \frac{R}{F}\right)$$

I skipped the intermittent steps to arrive at this point, but since we have been down this road so many times I trust the reader is now competent enough to recreate the necessary steps to arrive at this equation. We now substitute the equivalent statement for O, subscript 2C+1/F given before to find:

$$O_{\frac{2C+2}{F}} = O_{\frac{2C}{F}}\left(1 + \frac{R}{F}\right)\left(1 + \frac{R}{F}\right)$$

Thus at the second partitioned period after the second payment we have two groups of the parenthetic statement multiplied together; the definition of exponents. Extrapolating this observation carefully, we can clearly state that after some U amount of partitions pass, but before another payment, then a total of U parenthetic (1 + R/F) will be multiplied into the equation for the amount owed at period 2C/F. Mathematically this is written as:

$$O_{\frac{2C+U}{F}} = O_{\frac{2C}{F}}\left(1 + \frac{R}{F}\right)^{U}$$

$$= \left[P\left(1 + \frac{R}{F}\right)^{2C} - B\left(1 + \frac{R}{F}\right)^{C} - B\right]\left(1 + \frac{R}{F}\right)^{U}$$

$$= P\left(1 + \frac{R}{F}\right)^{2C+U} - B\left(1 + \frac{R}{F}\right)^{C+U} - B\left(1 + \frac{R}{F}\right)^{U}$$

Which is found directly by multiplying O, subscript 2C/F, by (1 + R/F) a total of U times to represent the passing of U partitioned time periods. If we wished to now approach the third payment time period then we could easily use the same logic we used before to determine the amount owed at the second payment period. Namely we allow U to equal another C and then subtract another payment:

$$O_{\frac{3C}{F}} = P\left(1 + \frac{R}{F}\right)^{3C} - B\left(1 + \frac{R}{F}\right)^{2C} - B\left(1 + \frac{R}{F}\right)^{C} - B$$

A glance at our evolving formula we may start to feel overwhelmed with the ever growing amount of terms we need to keep track of. One method to cut down on the amount of written terms included in the equation is the sigma summation developed in chapter 6. The opportunity for using the sigma summation rests in the payment application terms, thus our focus should start there:

$$-B\left(1+\frac{R}{F}\right)^{2C} - B\left(1+\frac{R}{F}\right)^{C} - B$$

The reader may quickly notice that each B is multiplied by an exponential parenthesis. The first B is coupled with a parenthesis raised to the power 2C, the second is raised to 1C. One may think that there is no exponential multiple in the third B, but if we wanted to get fancy we could actually define the third B to be multiplied by an exponential parenthesis raised to the 0C.

$$-B = -B\left(1+\frac{R}{F}\right)^{0C}$$

We know this to be true since this was covered in equation 3.5. Thus we really have three products of B with a descending exponential interest accumulation. But yet, other than this small change in the exponent, each of the three terms contains the exact same basic form. This fact gives us a readily observable pattern that we can easily transfer into a sigma summation with an upper bound of 2 and a lower bound of 0.

$$\sum_{k=0}^{2} -B\left(1+\frac{R}{F}\right)^{Ck}$$

And using equation 6.1 allows us to remove the constant coefficient (in terms of k!) from the summation.

$$-B\sum_{k=0}^{2}\left(1+\frac{R}{F}\right)^{Ck}$$

Now that we have successfully rewritten our string of addition into a concise summation, we should return to our main goal and finish deriving the general formula for dynamic compound interest with frequency. Using the notation above in our current general formula for time period 3C/F we find:

$$O_{\frac{3C}{F}} = P\left(1+\frac{R}{F}\right)^{3C} - B\sum_{k=0}^{2}\left(1+\frac{R}{F}\right)^{Ck}$$

Before moving on, it would be worth our time to revisit the equation for the 2Cth time frame and try to write it with a sigma summation. Recall that this was given as:

$$O_{\frac{2C}{F}} = P\left(1+\frac{R}{F}\right)^{2C} - B\left(1+\frac{R}{F}\right)^{C} - B$$

And re-writing the two terms at the end of the right hand side to reflect the sigma summation principals we discussed before we have:

$$O_{\frac{2C}{F}} = P\left(1 + \frac{R}{F}\right)^{2C} - B\sum_{k=0}^{1}\left(1 + \frac{R}{F}\right)^{Ck}$$

This form of the 2C/F time frame is very similar to the form for the 3C/F time frame. Perhaps we might pick apart a pattern by comparing these two equations that would give us a sufficient pattern that we could extrapolate to an appropriate general formula. First, notice that the first term, with a multiple of P, contains an exponent raised to the current time partition. Next, notice that a sigma summation follows with the exact same format in both the 2C/F and 3C/F time frame. The only difference being the upper index of the summation! The 2C/F partition's upper index is a one while the 3C/F is two. Thus the pattern that we see is that the upper index is one less than the number multiplied by C. Using all this information we can confidently write that any time period that is a multiple of C can be written as:

Equation 8.7

$$O_{\frac{nC}{F}} = P\left(1 + \frac{R}{F}\right)^{nC} - B\sum_{k=0}^{n-1}\left(1 + \frac{R}{F}\right)^{kC}$$

This equation represents the general formula for dynamic compound interest with frequency at any multiple of period C/F. Since we have defined C/F to be the first payment period, and since the payment is time repetitive, we can be sure that a multiple of C/F represents how many payments have been made. Thus our equation 8.7 above dictates the money owed at any payment period.

One will recall, however, that the compounding frequency was assumed to be much faster than the payment cycle. As such, our general equation fails to encompass the behavior of the loan during the frequency periods that exist between payment periods. But do we really care? The answer to this question is it depends on what you are trying to do. This book only seeks to derive a workable equation of the dynamic compound interest with frequency, which we have. As long as we are content with knowing how much is owed at the moment a payment is processed then we have come as far as we need to.

For those students who are not satisfied and wish to know the general equation for any frequency period then I would suggest reading about discrete mathematics. The reason behind this is that each period brings about a non-continuous change in the value of the equation. This change is not gradual but catastrophic. This means that before the partitioned period ends the value of the amount owed maintains a steady constant value. No matter how long this partitioned period is, the value will remain unchanged. Immediately after the period ends, however, there will be an instantaneous change in the amount owed from the effect of the payment, the interest accumulation, or both. This fact makes it impossible to continually map the amount owed mathematically. Because of this property, I will simply allow our progress to be sufficient for our purposes and end the derivation. But if you are interested in expanding on the understanding then I wholeheartedly applaud your enthusiasm. You should have all of the tools you need to derive a general equation between payment periods. Good Luck!

Hopefully you are now convinced that our equation still fully describes the process of dynamic compound interest with frequency in the general sense. But we aren't finished yet, that summation notation looks just like the extended geometric sequence in equation 6.9, repeated below for your convenience:

$$\sum_{L=0}^{m} j^{LC} = \frac{1 - j^{(m+1)C}}{1 - j^C}$$

If we now matched up our desired parameters, meaning we let (n-1) equal m, j equal (1 + R/F), L equal k, and C equal C, then we could easily create a simplification for the equation that specifies the amount owed at time period nC/F

Equation 8.8

$$O_{n\frac{C}{F}} = P\left(1 + \frac{R}{F}\right)^{nC} - B\left[\frac{1 - \left(1 + \frac{R}{F}\right)^{nC}}{1 - \left(1 + \frac{R}{F}\right)^{C}}\right]$$

And finally we have arrived at the simplified and generalized governing equation for dynamic compound interest with frequency at the time of payment assuming a payment is submitted every cth partitioned time period.

One should remember though that this section necessarily needs a partitioned frequency rate that is faster than the payment rate. If not then our initial assumptions while deriving the governing equations were unfounded and we are incorrect in our conclusions.

Section 8.6 – Special Cases of Dynamic Compounding Interest with Frequency:

This section is included to deal with three very important special cases of the general equation derived during the last section: when C is equal to F.

Case 1:

One possible scenario that correlates with this condition is when both C and F occur simultaneously during each time period. We could therefore correctly interpret this condition to coincide with a dynamic compound interest WITHOUT frequency because that derivation was performed by assuming both interest and payment were applied with each passing period. We could prove this mathematically by simply stating that C = F = 1. Substituting unity into every C and F in the general equation we find:

$$O_{\frac{n1}{1}} = P\left(1 + \frac{R}{1}\right)^{1n} - B\left[\frac{1 - \left(1 + \frac{R}{1}\right)^{1n}}{1 - \left(1 + \frac{R}{1}\right)^{1}}\right]$$

Using the various mathematical skills we have developed throughout this book that deal with the properties of unity we can simplify this equation to:

$$O_n = P(1 + R)^n + B\left[\frac{1 - (1 + R)^n}{R}\right]$$

Exactly as we expected! This equation that popped out of our assumption that C = F = 1 is exactly the same as the equation derived in equation 8.2 during the dynamic compound interest section without frequency. This result gives us a great deal of faith in the consistency of our derivations and should give you that warm tummy feeling that we are on the right track.

Case 2:

Another way for C to be equal to the value of F is when the interest rate's full period coincides with the payment period. For instance, consider a dynamic compound loan with frequency whose interest and payment rate are quoted at a yearly interval rate. With this information we can clearly state that no matter what the frequency is, it will progress through all of the intermittent partitions at the end of the year by definition. Thus F partitions must have transpired. Couple this with the fact that the payment will be paid on an annual basis, as per the supposal above, and we can state that the Cth time period necessarily has to coincide with the Fth partitioned time period. Hence C = F and equation 8.8 can be written as:

$$O_{n\frac{F}{F}} = P\left(1 + \frac{R}{F}\right)^{nF} - B\left[\frac{1 - \left(1 + \frac{R}{F}\right)^{nF}}{1 - \left(1 + \frac{R}{F}\right)^{F}}\right]$$

Case 3:

A very similar, but much more interesting case stems from letting F become very close to infinity. The logic behind this goes as such. Consider a yearly interest rate that we wish to cut up into a million partitioned periods that correspond with each interest accumulation. This scenario would mean that interest accrues on the loan once every 31 seconds! (31.536 seconds actually) It would seem ludicrous to bring a payment to the lender every two or three portioned periods. That would be like delivering a check every 1 to 2 minutes, day and night, 24 hours a day, 365 days a year. Forget about it, it's humanly impossible. Obviously the borrower would just settle with procuring a payment at a reasonable rate of say, once a week or once a month. If we were to assume the borrower paid each month, then this means that an average of 83333, give or take, partitioned periods pass in between each payment period. If we decided to let the frequency equal a billion or a trillion rather than a million then obviously the amount of periods that pass between each payment would increase as well since we have to fit more partitions into the same amount of actual time. Thus if we let F become very close to infinity, then C would naturally tend towards infinity as well and our special case condition will be met; F = C

This condition correlates with equation 8.8 written as:

$$\lim_{F \to \infty} O_{n\frac{F}{F}} =$$

$$P \lim_{F \to \infty} \left(1 + \frac{R}{F}\right)^{Fn} - B\left[\frac{1 - \lim_{F \to \infty} \left(1 + \frac{R}{F}\right)^{Fn}}{1 - \lim_{F \to \infty} \left(1 + \frac{R}{F}\right)^{F}}\right]$$

Then using the definition of Euler's constant for the parenthetic statements as F approaches infinity we find

Equation 8.9

$$O_n = Pe^{Rn} - B\frac{1 - e^{Rn}}{1 - e^{R}}$$

This equation is the result for dynamic continuous compounding interest, a very important equation as it dictates what the maximum amount of money is that can be owed at each payment period n for a given P, R, and B.

To a well versed mathematician, the equation corresponding to each special case speaks volumes about the behavior of the compound interest rates as affected by frequency. But some readers may not be as numerically inclined to understand just how devastating an increase in frequency can be.

As a conceptual illustration, let's suppose we encountered a loan with an agreed upon frequency of two. Let's further suppose, for purposes of our example, that the burrower can only afford to pay off the accumulated interest each time period. Under this assumption we can clearly state that the principal will never be touched and it will remain intact throughout the foreseeable future since the borrower is never reducing the original principal amount. In other words, the amount owed will remain constant for the foreseeable future.

Now let's assume that we want to mathematically analyze how these exact same circumstances (the interest rate, payment, and original principal of the previously discussed loan – whatever they may be) would react to a change in frequency set at one and infinity respectively. Conceptually the behavior of the loan could be mapped like so:

Figure 8.2

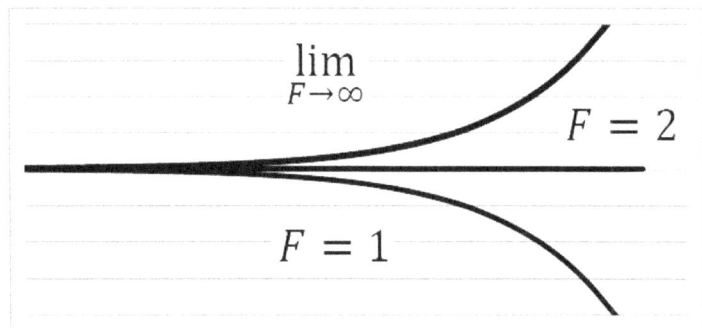

As can be seen by the illustration, and by our argument above, the loan with a frequency of 2 will remain unchanged through time. If however we maintained the same payment, but reduced the frequency to one, then mathematically we would begin to chip away at the total amount owed and will eventually pay the full loan off. But, if we maintained the same payment but increased the frequency to infinity, then the amount we owe would actually increase each time period despite the punctual payment by the borrower and we will be stuck on the upper most curve in the figure above. Hopefully figure 8.2 will serve to further reinforce the importance of frequency in compound interest. Numerical examples will be provided at the end of the chapter to numerically compare the effect of frequency as well.

This concludes the derivation of the general interest equations. Next chapter we will use our hard fought results to solve for the number of payments, and the size of payment needed, to completely satisfy the loan.

Section 8.7 – Numerical Examples
Example 8.1 – Evaluate the definition of Euler's constant given in equation 8.5 for R equal to 1 and F equal to 10, 100, 1000, 10000

-   Equation 8.5 is listed as

$$\lim_{F \to \infty} \left(1 + \frac{R}{F}\right)^F = e^R$$

- To evaluate at a specific F, we are allowed to remove the limit portion of the equation as long we replace the equal sign with an 'almost equal' sign. This reduces our equation to:

$$\left(1 + \frac{R}{F}\right)^F \approx e^R$$

- With R equal to 1, as given in the formulation of the problem, the equation becomes

$$\left(1 + \frac{1}{F}\right)^F \approx e^1$$

- Our first task is to set F equal to 10

$$\left(1 + \frac{1}{10}\right)^{10} \approx e$$

- Recalling that e is equal to 2.71828…, and then performing the calculation on the left hand side we get:

$$2.5937 … \approx 2.71828 …$$

- As you can see, the first approximation is off by two tenths.
- Moving on to F equal to 100

$$\left(1 + \frac{1}{100}\right)^{100} \approx e$$

- Performing the calculations gives
-

$$2.70481 … \approx 2.71828 …$$

- Now we are within two hundredths! Moving to F equal to 1000

$$\left(1 + \frac{1}{1000}\right)^{1000} \approx e$$

- And performing the calculations we find:

$$2.71692 … \approx 2.71828 …$$

- This value for F has brought our approximation to within 2 thousandths of the actual value for e. As we can see, a larger value of F seems to produce a more reliable approximate. Moving to our last supposal for F

$$\left(1 + \frac{1}{10000}\right)^{10000} \approx e$$

- And performing the calculation gives:

$$2.71814 … \approx 2.71828$$

- And we have a closer approximate value still at within 15 ten-thousandths of the original value
- This continual increase in the exactness of the approximation that we have just witnessed is called convergence.
- From this observation, it isn't so farfetched to think that as we approach infinity, meaning as F climbs higher and higher up the positive number tower, our approximation will become closer and closer to the value of e.
- Try a few larger numbers at your convenience to see this trend continue.

Example 8.2 – Compute the amount owed after 10 time periods for a static continuously compounded interest loan of 10000 units of currency at a 5 percent interest rate. Repeat the problem for a static compound interest loan without frequency and a static simple interest loan

- The continuously compounded interest is governed by equation 8.6

$$O_n = Pe^{Rn}$$

- To use R in our calculation, it must be in decimal format.

$$\frac{5}{100} = .05$$

- Thus R is equal to .05. The example also specifies that n equals 10 and P is equal to 10000. Plugging these numbers into the governing equation gives:

$$O_{10} = 16487.21$$

- Moving to the next part of the problem, static compound interest without frequency is given by equation 8.1

$$O_n = P(1 + R)^n$$

- Setting n to 10, P to 10000 and R to .05 and then computing yields:

$$O_{10} = 16228.95$$

- A can be seen, continuously compounding has resulted in an additional 250 units of interest accumulation relative to compound interest without frequency.
- The next part of the problem asks for the calculation for static simple interest
- Recall that static simple interest is governed by equation 7.2

$$o_n = p + prn$$

- With p equal to 10000, r equal to .05 and n equal to 10, the static simple interest yields:

$$O_n = 15000$$

- A reduction of 1228.95 and 1487.21 from the compound and continuous compound interests respectively.

Example 8.3 – How much is owed on the 12th time period for a 1000 unit loan at a 5 percent compound interest rate and payment of 20 units per time period.

- The governing equation for dynamic compound without frequency is given by equation 8.2

$$O_n = P(1 + R)^n + B\frac{1 - (1 + R)^n}{R}$$

- Letting n equal 12, p equal 1000, r equal $5/100 = .05$, and b = 20, the amount owed is calculated as:

$$O_{12} = 1477.51$$

- Notice that this is actually larger than the original principal of 1000.
- Thus the borrower has paid 20 units of currency 12 times and still owes more than he started with!
- The reason behind this is because the original accumulation of interest was given by

$$I_1 = pr = 50$$

- Since the payment was less than the actual interest accrual then the amount of money owed increased. This was then compounded with the next interest accumulation and caused the total amount owed to explode despite the payment by the burrower.
- This unfortunate situation occurs in the real world in the form of some credit card bills. The minimum payment is sometimes set below the interest accrual leading some borrowers to unknowingly enter this quagmire.

Example 8.4 – Repeat example 2.4 but set the payment to 50 units.

- Repeating the same calculations as before, but this time with b equal to 50 instead of 20, we find:

$$O_{12} = 1000$$

- Which is exactly the amount the borrower owed at the beginning of the loan.
- Thus the borrower has paid 50 units 12 times to still owe the same amount of money. Effectively the borrower is running in place and providing free money to the lender every time period.
- The reason for this is because, as argued in the last example, the interest accrual for the first time period is 50 units. When the borrower pays back 50 units he has essentially satisfied the accumulated interest and is back to the original principal. Another time period passing causes another interest accumulation of 50 units. Thus only paying the interest accrual in compound interest will cause the borrower to perpetually pay the lender forever.

Example 8.5 – Perform example 8.4 again but set the payment equal to 100
- Performing the calculation as in example 8.4 but setting the payment b equal to 100 produces:

$$O_{12} = 204.14$$

- The borrower has almost completely paid of the loan with this set of conditions

- The reason is because the payment of 100 units overcomes the initial interest accrual of 50 units and reduces the principal. Couple this with the fact that the interest accumulation necessarily decreases when the principal decreases and the borrower can take successively larger chunks out of the principal with each payment.
- Obviously this is the type of situation the borrower would like to be in.

Example 8.6 – Compute the amount owed at the 90th time period for a compounded interest loan at an interest rate of .05, a principal of 10000 units, and a payment of 512 units per period. Set the Frequency to 1, 2, 5, and infinite

- The governing equation for this example is given by equation 8.8

$$O_{n\frac{C}{F}} = P\left(1 + \frac{R}{F}\right)^{nC} - B\left[\frac{1 - \left(1 + \frac{R}{F}\right)^{nC}}{1 - \left(1 + \frac{R}{F}\right)^{C}}\right]$$

- One assumption that we can quickly make is that F must equal C. The reasoning for this is that we can assume that the full interest period coincides with the payment period. Thus we match the special case scenario presented in case two of section 8.6
- R is given as .05 in the instructions, and it is already in decimal format so we don't need to do anything to it.
- P is also given in the starting paragraph at a value of 10000.
- B is given as 512
- Let's assume F to be 1, and since a full payment period is covered by one installment of the frequency then C is 1 as well.
- Plugging these values into the 90th time period we find:

$$O_{90} = -9135.29$$

- Setting the Performing the same operation except for F and C equal to 2

$$O_{90} = 439.74$$

- Again performing the same calculation except changing F and C to 5

$$O_{90} = 6759.29$$

- Finally taking F and C to be infinity we may utilize equation 8.9, or case 3 of section 8.6

$$O_n = Pe^{Rn} - B\frac{1 - e^{Rn}}{1 - e^{R}}$$

- Plugging in the assumed values for the variables we find:

$$O_{90} = 11234.38$$

- As can be seen, the frequency can greatly impact the remaining debt.

Example 8.7 – Consider a compound interest loan with monthly frequency for 2329.62 units of currency. The interest rate was agreed to be .12 per annum. If the monthly payment B equals 70.95, how much is still owed after the end of 40 months?

- Our time period setting for this example will be on a monthly basis. Thus the interest rate must be modified to match our time period. A year contains twelve months, thus:

$$\frac{.12}{12} = .01$$

- P equals 2329.62, B equals 70.95, and n equals 40 as per the instructions
- A question may remain for which equation to use for this example. The instructions inform us that the type of loan considered is compound interest with frequency. But recall that the current period was dictated by the payments occurrence. Since we have a monthly payment, the frequency of the interest accumulation coincides with the payment.
- The beauty of the mathematics of interest is that we could potentially use equation 8.2 or 8.8, provided we conform the variables to fit their assumptions
- For instance, if we wished to use equation 8.2

$$O_n = P(1 + R)^n + B\frac{1 - (1 + R)^n}{R}$$

- Then we would need R to be configured into its monthly decimal format, or R equal .01. Plugging in the values for each of the variables produces:

$$O_{40} = 0$$

- This result means that the entire loan has been paid off. The borrower now owes the lender nothing and the loan has been satisfied
- If we, however, wished to use equation 8.8

$$O_{n\frac{C}{F}} = P\left(1 + \frac{R}{F}\right)^{nC} - B\left[\frac{1 - \left(1 + \frac{R}{F}\right)^{nC}}{1 - \left(1 + \frac{R}{F}\right)^{C}}\right]$$

- Then we would need to define R, F, and C.
- Since this equation takes into account the full value of R in its assumptions, R will equal .12.
- F is given in the instructions as monthly, therefore 12
- C is determined by the number of partitioned periods that pass before a payment is received. Since the payment is monthly and the frequency is set a monthly, we know that only one partitioned period passes each payment. Thus C = 1
- The variable n, we will recall, tallies the number of payments processed, thus at 40 months 40 payments have been processed.
- Plugging this into the equation we find:

$$O_{40\frac{1}{12}} = 0$$

- It seems as if we got extremely lucky by picking this certain set of variables that just so happened to satisfy the loan, but is there a way to do this on purpose? Is there a way to find the specific variables necessary to satisfy the loan?
- That's a good question, and one we will explore in the next section.

Chapter 9 – Expanding on the Governing Equations

Through this text we have successfully navigated the various modes of interest accumulation and derived each of the governing equations. These governing equations were provided in the context of the amount owed at a respective period. But there is other information that we could glean from the governing mathematical behavior of interest. For instance, suppose we wanted to know how many payments are necessary to pay off a loan. Or how large of a payment will be necessary to eliminate the loan. Or what is the total amount of money that will be paid over the life of the loan. Luckily all of this information can be found through the governing equations of interest. We only need to focus our attention and apply the methods developed in section 5.6 and maintain equality as we manipulate the equation to procure our desired information.

Algebra has the very real limitation of only being able to determine the unknown value of one variable for each equation. Thus for all of these 'solutions' we will assume that you have firm knowledge of all other variables contained in the equation. As an example, the previous chapters on interest assumed that the principal, interest rate, time period, and payment amount were all known to construct the amount owed. If any of these variables were not given or could not be procured through other methods then the actual numerical value of the amount owed could not be determined. This does not mean that we could not theoretically approach the problem, because that is exactly what we did through the chapter's derivations. It only means that we can't produce an actual numerical answer to a set of conditions without knowing the actual conditions.

Without further ado, let us begin our exploration into the governing equations of interest. To start, we will approach the less complex static interest before we attempt the more difficult dynamic interest.

Section 9.1 – The Static Simple Interest

The static simple interest's behavior was found to be governed by equation 7.2:

$$o_n = p(1 + nr)$$

Recall that the variable o stood for money owed, p for the principal, n for the number of time periods passed, and r for the interest rate. At this point the equation is explicitly solved for the variable o, money owed. We call this explicitly solved because o is isolated on one side of the equation without any other o on the other side of the equation. Being solved explicitly gives the advantage of being able to determine the numerical value of o by simply plugging in values for the other variables. This was accomplished in the numerical examples in the simple interest section

In our current state our governing equation is tuned, so to speak, for determining the amount owed when provided with the principal, interest rate, and number of passed periods. But suppose we already knew the desired amount owed and wanted to know how many passed periods, what interest rate, or starting principal would be necessary to achieve this given o. How would we go about doing this?

One method is to manipulate the equation in such a way to isolate a needed variable. Equality must be maintained throughout this process however, lest we lose the truth of our governing equation. Fortunately we already developed the necessary skills to do this in section 5.6. Our goal now is to solve the governing equation for each of the other variables explicitly, meaning that the variable is individually isolated on one side of the equation while maintaining the equality. Let's first begin by solving for the principal explicitly. To do this we divide both sides by the parenthetic statement of 1 + nr.

$$\frac{o_n}{(1+nr)} = \frac{p(1+nr)}{(1+nr)}$$

Notice that we may divide out the common factor on the right hand side by equation 2.13. Although one might think that this is not allowed because of the addition, we are taking the parenthesis as a whole to be our variable. This produces

Equation 9.1
$$\frac{o_n}{(1+nr)} = p$$

And we have successfully solved explicitly for p. If we were to have all information for amount owed, number of months, and the rate then we could use this equation to solve for the original principal amount of the loan.

Moving on, we have two other variables to solve for, n and r. Let's focus on n first. Starting with the governing equation:

$$o_n = p(1+nr)$$

Our first task is to move the principal to the other side of the equation. This can easily be accomplished by dividing both sides by p.

$$\frac{o_n}{p} = \frac{p(1+nr)}{p}$$

Simplifying the right hand side by dividing out the common p's we will find:

$$\frac{o_n}{p} = 1 + nr$$

To continue in our goal, we now need to subtract one from both sides. This will isolate the product nr on the right hand side of the equation.

$$\frac{o_n}{p} - 1 = 1 + nr - 1$$

Obviously, subtracting one from one will eliminate both of the ones on the right.

$$\frac{o_n}{p} - 1 = nr$$

Now we simply divide everything by r and we will have explicitly solved for n.

Equation 9.2
$$\frac{o_n}{rp} - \frac{1}{r} = n$$

This equation is explicitly solved for n, which you will recall means that n is isolated on one side of the equation. Thus if we have the principal, interest rate, and amount owed we could easily figure out the number of periods that have passed by utilizing this equation. Some may protest that we haven't really solved explicitly for n since there is still an n residing in the subscript of the variable o. Although a true observation, this n isn't a true variable and is instead used to differentiate the amount owed in this nth time period from the other time periods. It is a specifying component of a variable and therefore not a true variable. Hopefully this clears up any confusion.

The last variable to solve for is the variable r. But let's not start with the governing equation. Instead, let's capitalize on the fact that we nearly isolated r while solving for n explicitly. This was given by:

$$\frac{o_n}{p} - 1 = nr$$

Now since we have maintained equality at all times by performing the exact same operations on both sides of the equation, we can truthfully say that this equation holds as much mathematical fact as any of the other derived equations. With this in mind, we simply need to divide both sides by n to isolate r on one side of the equation.

Equation 9.3

$$\frac{o_n}{pn} - \frac{1}{n} = r$$

And equation 9.3 above directly determines a needed interest rate to satisfy a known principal, period, and amount owed.

Section 9.2 - The Static Compound Interest:

The governing equation for the static compound interest was derived as equation 8.1:

$$O_n = P(1 + R)^n$$

This equation can be interpreted as being solved explicitly for the money owed at any time period n. Our goal now is to solve for each of the other variables just as we did for static simple interest. First up, let's solve for P by simply dividing everything that isn't P from the right hand side of the equation. Doing this provides:

Equation 9.4

$$\frac{O_n}{(1 + R)^n} = P$$

Solving for n is a little more intense. But that shouldn't stop us. First thing we should do is to divide both sides of the governing equation by P. This produces:

$$\frac{O_n}{P} = (1 + R)^n$$

At this point we notice that n is actually an exponent. We will need a way to dissociate the exponent from its parenthetic base before we can hope to progress forward in solving explicitly for n. Luckily, we have already developed a way to interact with exponents: the logarithm. This is the first time we will use the logarithm rules that we developed in chapter 4. Thus to begin we must take the logarithm of both sides to find:

$$\ln \frac{O_n}{P} = ln(1 + R)^n$$

Now we could easily use the results of equation 4.7 to pull the n out of the exponent.

$$\ln \frac{O_n}{P} = n ln(1 + R)$$

As an added simplification, let's also utilize equation 4.6 to change the left hand side of the equation into a subtraction.

$$\ln O_n - \ln P = n \ln(1 + R)$$

Now we simply divide both sides by the logarithm on the right hand side to isolate our variable n:

Equation 9.5

$$\frac{\ln O_n - \ln P}{\ln(1 + R)} = n$$

And we have solved explicitly for n.

The last variable that needs to be addressed is the interest rate R. Let us again begin with the governing equation of static compound interest:

$$O_n = P(1 + R)^n$$

Again, our goal is to strip away all of the excess variables until we can isolate R on one side of the equation. The first step would be to divide both sides by P. Doing so, and making the necessary simplifications, will produce:

$$\frac{O_n}{P} = (1 + R)^n$$

Since we are presently trying to isolate the variable R, we must figure out a way to nullify the variable n. But didn't we develop a method known as the radical in chapter 3 that did just this? Applying the results of section 3.6 we take the nth radical of both sides of the equation.

$$\left(\frac{O_n}{P}\right)^{\frac{1}{n}} = (1 + R)^{\frac{n}{n}}$$

Now we can reduce the exponent on the right hand side of the equation by the divisional property of unity. This gives:

$$\left(\frac{O_n}{P}\right)^{\frac{1}{n}} = 1 + R$$

The parentheses have been omitted from the right hand side of the equation since they are no longer needed. To complete our task, we only need to subtract both sides by 1.

$$\left(\frac{O_n}{P}\right)^{\frac{1}{n}} - 1 = 1 + R - 1$$

Of course we could easily combine both the positive and negative one producing

Equation 9.6

$$\left(\frac{O_n}{P}\right)^{\frac{1}{n}} - 1 = R$$

And we have now solved the static compound interest for the interest rate R. This concludes the exploration of the governing equations of static interest. Moving on we now approach the dynamic interests which contain an added level of complexity due to the payment variable B.

Section 9.3 – Satisfying Dynamic Interest Loans:

This section will approach the process of solving for each variable a little differently than before because dynamic interest is concerned with a payments effect upon an outstanding principal. Our new goal will be to determine the necessary criteria to satisfy a loan holding. For sake of accessibility and ease, we will only trouble ourselves with one variable at a time and assume all other variables as constant.

Section 9.4 – Special Case of Dynamic Simple Interest:

Recall that if we allowed the assumption that the critical time period was equal to the ratio of p/b, then the Dynamic Simple interest loan was found to be governed by equation 7.4 before the critical time period and equation 7.8 after.

$$o_n = \begin{cases} p - nb + prn - \dfrac{brn(n-1)}{2}; & n < \dfrac{p}{b} + 1 \\ p - nb + \dfrac{p^2 r}{2b} + \dfrac{pr}{2}; & n \geq \dfrac{p}{b} + 1 \end{cases}$$

One of the more interesting tasks, from a utilitarian perspective, is to find the payment amount necessary to pay off a loan within a given number of time periods. This can be found by solving the governing equation explicitly for b, which was the variable we used to represent the size of the payment. But wait, we have two governing equations for dynamic simple interest. So which one of the two should serve as a starting point to determine the payment size necessary to eliminate the debt?

This little conundrum can be quickly dispatched by applying a little logic. Our stated goal is to eliminate the debt, meaning that we owe nothing. It stands to reason that satisfying the total debt would require not only repayment of the principal but also enough payment to cover all accrued interest. Now since the definition of the critical time period specified the moment of satisfying all outstanding principal, we can clearly state that eliminating all debt would necessarily place us beyond the critical time period. Thus our focus should rest in the second governing equation of dynamic simple interest.

$$o_n = p - nb + \frac{p^2 r}{2b} + \frac{pr}{2}$$

$$n \geq \frac{P}{B} + 1$$

Finally, since we wish to eliminate the debt, we know that the variable o, subscript n, will have to be zero because we must owe nothing for the debt to be satisfied.

Equation 9.7

$$0 = p - nb + \frac{p^2r}{2b} + \frac{pr}{2}$$

Be sure to recognize that the left hand side of the equation is not the variable o, subscript n, but the number zero. Now that we have both chosen and simplified our governing equation to reflect that the full loan has been reduced to zero, we may begin our derivation to explicitly solve for the variable b.

As we look at our equation, we should notice that b is in the numerator of the term nb and in the denominator in the following term. This will cause some trouble for us so it would be best if the first thing we did was to get rid of fractions. We can easily do this by multiplying both sides by 2b:

$$2b(0) = \left(p - nb + \frac{p^2r}{2b} + \frac{pr}{2} \right) 2b$$

At this point we will need to distribute the 2b to each term within the parenthesis. Carrying this out, as well as eliminating the divisor lines by use of equation 2.13, we will have

$$0 = 2bp - 2nb^2 + p^2r + bpr$$

For reasons that will be revealed to you in a bit we are going to rearrange this equation to a more suiting form. First we will need to multiply both sides by negative one. This will result in changing each term from positive to negative and vice versa.

$$0 = -2bp + 2nb^2 - p^2r - bpr$$

And of course a negative zero is still zero so the left hand side will not change sign. Now that this is accomplished, we will also need to place the b squared term closest to the equals sign, the two b terms after, and the term without a b last. This is accomplished by invoking the commutative property of addition.

$$0 = 2nb^2 - 2bp - bpr - p^2r$$

Now we will pull out the common b from the two middle terms by the distributive property in reverse.

$$0 = 2nb^2 - (2p + pr)b - p^2r$$

The form of the equation you see presently is just as valid as what we started out with in the governing equation. We know this to be true because we have only utilized mathematical processes that maintain equality throughout the operation. Although exactly equal to equation 9.7, this form of the equation contains an added bonus because it is written as a quadratic equation as explored in section 5.7.

$$Wx^2 + Yx + Z = 0$$

This helps us immensely because the quadratic equation contains a trusted solution. Utilizing the quadratic formula, equation 5.9, we can solve explicitly for b:

$$b = \frac{-Y + [Y^2 - 4WZ]^{\frac{1}{2}}}{2W}$$

Thus application of the quadratic formula is an exercise in plugging the appropriate mathematical statements at the appropriate locations. Comparing the necessary equations we notice that if we list the following substitutions:

$$W = 2n$$
$$Y = -(2p + pr)$$
$$Z = -p^2 r$$

Then our quadratic equation in b would match the necessary requirements for the quadratic formula. Thus we merely need to substitute these expressions into the quadratic formula and we will have solved for b. Doing this we find:

Equation 9.8

$$b = \frac{2p + pr + [(2p + pr)^2 + 8np^2 r]^{\frac{1}{2}}}{4n}$$

This equation provides the amount of money that needs to be paid to completely eliminate debt in the dynamic simple interest case assuming that p, r, and n are given.

Moving on, it is time that we address the variable p. Solving explicitly for the amount of principal required to satisfy all debt, provided we know b, r, and n, will prove to be very similar to the approach we took for b above. First applying the restriction that the variable o, subscript n, is zero we find equation 9.7:

$$0 = p - nb + \frac{p^2 r}{2b} + \frac{pr}{2}$$

Now, as a simplification tool, let's multiply both sides by 2b again so that we can clear fractions from the equation.

$$0 = 2bp - 2nb^2 + p^2 r + bpr$$

Upon inspection of the four additive terms, we notice that there is a term with p squared, two terms with p, and one term that does not contain p. Thus we have a quadratic equation. Rearranging the equation through the commutative property of addition allows us to align the terms in descending powers of p.

$$0 = p^2 r + 2bp + bpr - 2nb^2$$

One final adjustment is to pull out the common p between the two inner terms by the distributive property in reverse. And just for ease of recognition, let's also switch the order of the product in the first term.

$$0 = rp^2 + (2b + br)p - 2nb^2$$

Here stands a perfect example of the form of the quadratic equation. Using the substitutions of

$$r = W$$
$$(2b + br) = Y$$
$$-2nb^2 = Z$$

Our intended quadratic equation in variable p simply pops out of the page:

$$0 = Wp^2 + Yp + Z$$

Our only task now is to apply the quadratic formula, given by equation 5.9

$$p = \frac{-Y + [Y^2 - 4WZ]^{\frac{1}{2}}}{2W}$$

Plugging the equated values for W, Y, and Z and following the tenets of GLEMA we find:

Equation 9.9

$$p = \frac{-2b - br + [(2b + br)^2 + 8rnb^2]^{\frac{1}{2}}}{2r}$$

And we have explicitly solved the dynamic simple interest equation for p.

The next two variables we need to approach, n and r, are much simpler to isolate because we do not need to resort to the quadratic formula. Indeed the steps to explicitly solve for n will now feel like child's play. Let's us begin with the general governing equation for periods after the critical n and restrict our attention to the payoff of the debt. This gives us a starting point of equation 9.7:

$$0 = p - nb + \frac{p^2 r}{2b} + \frac{pr}{2}$$

Where again, the left hand side of the equation is the number zero to reflect that the entire loan has been settled. Careful inspection of equation 9.7 shows that there is only one variable n to contend with. Thus if we could isolate this term nb to one side of the equation then we would nearly be home free. After a little thought we decide the best bet will be to add nb to both sides. Doing so, and combining like terms, we have:

$$nb = p + \frac{p^2 r}{2b} + \frac{pr}{2}$$

Now all we need to do is to divide both sides by b.

Equation 9.10

$$n = \frac{p}{b} + \frac{p^2 r}{2b^2} + \frac{pr}{2b}$$

The variable n is now isolated and therefore solved explicitly. Assuming we know the values of p, b, and r, we can now easily use equation 9.10 above to determine the number of payment periods necessary to eliminate a loan.

Our last variable to solve explicitly for in the dynamic simple interest is r. So let's again begin by assuming that we are interested in finding the necessary r needed to eliminate a loan provided we are given distinct values for p, b, and n. Our best approach, due to reasons that have been exhaustively covered before, is to begin with equation 9.7

$$0 = p - nb + \frac{p^2 r}{2b} + \frac{pr}{2}$$

Inspecting our equation for a starting point we should notice that there are only two variable r's in the whole equation and both are in the numerator of the last two terms. One approach that could be taken is to subtract these two terms to the other side through the logic given in section 5.6. Accomplishing this task will produce:

$$-\frac{p^2 r}{2b} - \frac{pr}{2} = p - nb$$

Now we could easily factor out the common r using the distributive property in reverse.

$$r\left(-\frac{p^2}{2b} - \frac{p}{2}\right) = p - nb$$

At this point, we merely need to divide the left hand side by everything that IS NOT r. Of course to maintain equality we will need to perform the same operation to the right hand side as well.

$$\frac{r\left(-\frac{p^2}{2b} - \frac{p}{2}\right)}{\left(-\frac{p^2}{2b} - \frac{p}{2}\right)} = \frac{p - nb}{\left(-\frac{p^2}{2b} - \frac{p}{2}\right)}$$

The left hand side of the equation can be divided out to one to reduce the common parenthetic statement. This may seem surprising to some as the parenthetic statement is so big. The fact is that mathematics doesn't care. It is important to remember that we are dealing with some actual finite number that is represented by the parenthetic statement. Thus when this finite number is divided by itself, no matter what it looks like, the idea presented in the divisional property of unity remains intact. Once this division is reduced to one, we simply have r multiplied by 1 on the left hand side, which we will recall is r.

Equation 9.11

$$r = \frac{p - nb}{\left(-\frac{p^2}{2b} - \frac{p}{2}\right)}$$

Equation 9.11 above explicitly solves the settling of a dynamic simple interest loan for r. With this equation we can deduce the required r necessary to settle a loan provided we are given a specific p, b, and n.

Section 9.5 – General Dynamic Simple Interest:

The last section contained a highly selective assumption that n critical must equal p/b to maintain complete mathematical validity. This section will remove that requirement and will seek to solve explicitly for each of the variables of the general dynamic simple interest formula at resolution of debt. Recall that the generalized governing dynamic simple interest formula was given by equation 7.4 before the critical time period and equation 7.6 after:

$$o_n = \begin{cases} p - nb + prn - \dfrac{brn(n-1)}{2}; & n < \dfrac{p}{b} + 1 \\ p - nb + prn_c - \dfrac{brn_c(n_c - 1)}{2}; & n \geq \dfrac{p}{b} + 1 \end{cases}$$

Where n, subscript c, is known as the critical time period. Since we are again seeking to solve the equation at the elimination of the loan, we can use the same argument as last time to choose the second equation and set o, subscript n, to zero to reflect that we no longer owe any money:

Equation 9.12

$$0 = p - nb + prn_c - \frac{brn_c(n_c - 1)}{2}$$

Recall that the critical time period was defined as the largest integer that satisfied the first qualifier of being less than p/b +1. Recall further that this critical time period determined the total amount of interest accumulated over the life of the loan. Thus knowledge of the critical time period is vital to fully calculating a dynamic simple interest loan. If we already know both p and b, then we can quickly surmise the critical time period n, subscript c, and use it in our assumptions of known variables. For instance, assume we know r, b, and p, which also gives us knowledge of the critical time period. Further assume that we wish to solve explicitly for the variable n; the number of payment periods necessary to satisfy the loan. To isolate n, our first step will be to add the term nb to both sides. Doing so will eliminate it from the right hand side.

$$nb = p + prn_c - \frac{brn_c(n_c - 1)}{2}$$

Now we simple divide both sides by b to arrive at the solution for the variable n:

Equation 9.13

$$n = \frac{p}{b} + \frac{prn_c}{b} - \frac{rn_c(n_c - 1)}{2}$$

Notice that the b in the last term has been divided out. Equation 9.13 above does indeed solve explicitly for n because there are no other n on the right hand side of the equations. Some readers may protest that n, subscript c, is still an n, but you are missing the point. The critical time period is a completely different number than the pay off period, and thus the two variables are actually quite different in value and idea.

Let's move on to solving explicitly for the variable r. Beginning with our usual assumptions we find equation 9.12

$$0 = p - nb + prn_c - \frac{brn_c(n_c - 1)}{2}$$

Assuming we have knowledge of all other variables, and through that knowledge of p and b we can deduce the critical time period, our first step will be to move the two terms with an r to the other side of the equation.

$$\frac{brn_c(n_c - 1)}{2} - prn_c = p - nb$$

Pulling out the common r by the distributive property in reverse we find:

$$r\left(\frac{bn_c(n_c - 1)}{2} - pn_c\right) = p - nb$$

Now we simply divide both sides by what isn't r on the left hand side of the equation.

$$\frac{r\left(\frac{bn_c(n_c - 1)}{2} - pn_c\right)}{\left(\frac{bn_c(n_c - 1)}{2} - pn_c\right)} = \frac{p - nb}{\left(\frac{bn_c(n_c - 1)}{2} - pn_c\right)}$$

Dividing out the common variables on the left hand side of the equation we find:

Equation 9.14

$$r = \frac{p - nb}{\left(\frac{bn_c(n_c - 1)}{2} - pn_c \right)}$$

Which really wasn't that difficult now that we are finished. With these two variables out of the way we are only left with the payment amount, b, and the original principal, p. However, one will recall that these two variables are necessary to determine the critical time period n, subscript c. Thus without information on one of these variables the critical time period is a complete mystery and solving explicitly for either variable is a worthless, even impossible, endeavor. Unless we can find some way around this inconsistency then we are at an impasse.

Luckily there is a way around this problem. For reasons that go beyond the scope of this book, we can obtain an appropriate estimate of either p or b if we utilize equations 9.9 or 9.8 respectively. These equations, obtained during the section detailing the special case scenario, do not contain the critical time period variable and are immune to what ails us presently. Once we find this 'appropriate' approximation, then we can combine it with our prior knowledge to produce the actual critical time period. As stated before, the logic behind this ability goes beyond the scope of this text. But any interested student can find illuminated guidance by exploring discrete mathematics and linear approximations.

With the critical time period solved, we can refine our initial approximation by solving the general governing equation explicitly. First, let's solve for the principal. Beginning with equation 9.12.

$$0 = p - nb + prn_c - \frac{brn_c(n_c - 1)}{2}$$

Our first step is to remove everything that doesn't contain the variable p to the other side of the equation. This is accomplished by adding the second and fourth term to both sides of the equation resulting in:

$$\frac{brn_c(n_c - 1)}{2} + nb = p + prn_c$$

Now let's pull out the common p by the distributive property in reverse

$$\frac{brn_c(n_c - 1)}{2} + nb = p(1 + rn_c)$$

The left hand side of the equation could stand a little clean up. First we will combine the two terms into a common ratio using equation 5.6

$$\frac{brn_c(n_c - 1) + 2nb}{2} = p(1 + rn_c)$$

To isolate p, we simply divide both sides by everything that isn't p on the right hand side. Doing this produces

$$\frac{\frac{brn_c(n_c - 1) + 2nb}{2}}{(1 + rn_c)} = p$$

Utilizing equation 2.22 we find the explicit solution for the principal p.

Equation 9.15

$$\frac{brn_c(n_c - 1) + 2nb}{2(1 + rn_c)} = p$$

A similar method is used for the explicit solution of the payment b. First we must utilize the special case scenario to solve for a first approximation of b. Then we use this information to produce a critical time period with the known original principal. Once this is accomplished we will have all information necessary to explicitly solve for b. Starting with equation 9.12

$$0 = p - nb + prn_c - \frac{brn_c(n_c - 1)}{2}$$

Our first step is to get rid of the ratio by multiplying everything by 2

$$0 = 2p - 2nb + 2prn_c - brn_c(n_c - 1)$$

With this step completed, we notice that b is present in two terms. Adding both of these terms to both sides will eliminate all b's from the right hand side of the equation.

$$2nb - brn_c(n_c - 1) = 2p + 2prn_c$$

Using the distributive property in reverse we can pull out the common b

$$b[2n + rn_c(n_c - 1)] = 2p + 2prn_c$$

Now we simply divide both sides by everything that isn't b on the right hand side of the equation. This results in isolating b on one side of the equation.

Equation 9.16

$$b = \frac{2p + 2prn_c}{2n + rn_c(n_c - 1)}$$

Through this equation, we can calculate the necessary payment per period to completely satisfy the debt provided we know all the other variables.

Section 9.6 – Dynamic Compound Interest with Frequency

Proficiency in this section will prove to be critical as nearly all practical loans follow this model of dynamic compound interest accumulation. Furthermore, by hypothetically manipulating the relative sizes of the frequency F and the payment period C, we can use these results to spring board into both the continuous compounding interest as well as the less simple interest models. Therefore it is critical that we remain steadfast in our logic to produce absolutely correct conclusions during this section.

To begin, recall that we found the governing equation for the dynamic compound interest to be:

$$O_{\frac{nC}{F}} = P\left(1+\frac{R}{F}\right)^{nC} - B\left[\frac{1-\left(1+\frac{R}{F}\right)^{nC}}{1-\left(1+\frac{R}{F}\right)^{C}}\right]$$

Since we are dealing with a dynamic model, our goal will be to solve the various variables for the conditions necessary to pay off the loan. Thus we can substitute a zero for the variable O, subscript nC/F.

Equation 9.17

$$0 = P\left(1+\frac{R}{F}\right)^{nC} - B\left[\frac{1-\left(1+\frac{R}{F}\right)^{nC}}{1-\left(1+\frac{R}{F}\right)^{C}}\right]$$

Solving explicitly for the payment necessary to eliminate a loan is a very important piece of information for both parties. Thus let us turn our attention to how exactly this is done.

Luckily for us, there is only one variable b throughout the whole equation. Isolating this single b will prove to be relatively easy compared to what we have already been through. Our first step is to separate the two terms by adding the bracketed term to both sides. Carrying this out gives us:

$$B\left[\frac{1-\left(1+\frac{R}{F}\right)^{nC}}{1-\left(1+\frac{R}{F}\right)^{C}}\right] = P\left(1+\frac{R}{F}\right)^{nC}$$

At this point we can multiply both sides by the denominator of the left hand side. This will serve to eliminate the denominator.

$$B\left[1-\left(1+\frac{R}{F}\right)^{nC}\right] = P\left(1+\frac{R}{F}\right)^{nC}\left(1-\left(1+\frac{R}{F}\right)^{C}\right)$$

Now we merely need to divide the left hand side by everything that isn't B. Of course to maintain equality we must perform this operation to both sides of the equation.

Equation 9.18

$$B = P\left(1+\frac{R}{F}\right)^{nC}\left[\frac{1-\left(1+\frac{R}{F}\right)^{C}}{1-\left(1+\frac{R}{F}\right)^{nC}}\right]$$

And we have successfully isolated the variable B. Since we have only used three properties of equality, we can be sure that we haven't made a mistake and equation 9.18 above does indeed give the true value for B provided we know P, R, F, n, and C.

As mentioned before, this result can be used as a basis for the less simple and continuous compound interest. For instance, suppose we set C = F = 1 which correlates with the less simple interest requirements. Plugging this into the equation provides:

$$B = P(1+R)^n\left[\frac{1-(1+R)}{1-(1+R)^n}\right]$$

Combining like terms in the numerator

Equation 9.19

$$B = P(1+R)^n \left[\frac{-R}{1-(1+R)^n} \right]$$

And we have arrived at the mathematical statement that represents the payment required to pay off a loan with less simple interest.

If we instead wanted F in equation 9.18 to approach infinity which, as argued before, would also cause C to approach infinity then we would produce the requirements necessary for continuous compounding interest. Thus we would have:

$$B = P \lim_{F \to \infty} \left(1 + \frac{R}{F}\right)^{nF} \left[\frac{1 - \left(1 + \frac{R}{F}\right)^{F}}{1 - \left(1 + \frac{R}{F}\right)^{nF}} \right]$$

Now we apply the definition of Euler's constant from equation 8.5 and we reach the mathematical representation of the payment necessary to settle a continuously compounding loan provided we know R, N, and P.

Equation 9.20

$$B = Pe^{Rn} \left[\frac{1 - e^R}{1 - e^{Rn}} \right]$$

Now that the payment variable B has been taken care of, let's move our attention to the number of periods necessary to satisfy a dynamic compound interest debt. Starting with our equation 9.17:

$$0 = P\left(1 + \frac{R}{F}\right)^{nC} - B \left[\frac{1 - \left(1 + \frac{R}{F}\right)^{nC}}{1 - \left(1 + \frac{R}{F}\right)^{C}} \right]$$

Inspecting our equation, we notice that the variable n crops up in two places. Fortunately though, they are both in the exponent and we have an obvious plan of attack. Our mission is to use the property of logarithms to yank the exponent down just as was done while solving for n for the static compound interest. To do this of course, we must first isolate the parenthetic statement containing the variable n in the exponent. To the inexperienced this may seem like a very difficult proposition. But by now we should be very confident in our mathematical ability and should be able to tackle this easily. Or, if you still feel like you wouldn't be able to do it, at least you have all the tools necessary to understand the following argument.

First, let's place one of the terms on the other side of the equals sign by adding the bracketed term to both sides:

$$B \left[\frac{1 - \left(1 + \frac{R}{F}\right)^{nC}}{1 - \left(1 + \frac{R}{F}\right)^{C}} \right] = P\left(1 + \frac{R}{F}\right)^{nC}$$

The next step in the derivation is to multiply B into the numerator of the bracketed statement by equation 2.16

$$\frac{B - B\left(1+\frac{R}{F}\right)^{nC}}{1-\left(1+\frac{R}{F}\right)^{C}} = P\left(1+\frac{R}{F}\right)^{nC}$$

What is important to note is that all of the operations we use to explore the complex algebraic equations such as this have already been dealt with in the preceding chapters. Really we aren't doing anything new, only applying what we already know in small verifiable steps. Continuing, let's now multiply both sides by the denominator of the left hand side of the equation. This will cause the denominator to logically divide out, as shown by equation 2.13

$$B - B\left(1+\frac{R}{F}\right)^{nC} = \left[1-\left(1+\frac{R}{F}\right)^{C}\right]P\left(1+\frac{R}{F}\right)^{nC}$$

Now, let's add the parenthetic term from the left hand side of the equation to both sides. This will leave only b on the left hand side.

$$B = \left[1-\left(1+\frac{R}{F}\right)^{C}\right]P\left(1+\frac{R}{F}\right)^{nC} + B\left(1+\frac{R}{F}\right)^{nC}$$

Using the distributive property in reverse, we can remove the common parenthesis with an n in the exponent.

$$B = \left(P - P\left(1+\frac{R}{F}\right)^{C} + B\right)\left(1+\frac{R}{F}\right)^{nC}$$

Notice that the right hand side of the equation now consists of a product containing two parenthetic terms and one of these parenthesis is raised to the nth power. The other parenthesis, however, does not and it is extraneous information at this point. So let's divide both sides by the parenthetic statement that does not contain an n in the exponent so we can focus more easily on that which presently matters. Carrying out this operation leaves us with

$$\frac{B}{\left(P - P\left(1+\frac{R}{F}\right)^{C} + B\right)} = \left(1+\frac{R}{F}\right)^{nC}$$

At this point we have successfully isolated the parenthesis raised to a power of n. One easy method to set up the isolation of n, and one we have used before in the static compound interest section, is to take the natural logarithm of both sides.

$$\ln\frac{B}{\left(P - P\left(1+\frac{R}{F}\right)^{C} + B\right)} = \ln\left(1+\frac{R}{F}\right)^{nC}$$

Now we may use equation 4.7 to pull the n out of the exponent.

$$\ln \frac{B}{\left(P - P\left(1 + \frac{R}{F}\right)^C + B\right)} = n \ln\left(1 + \frac{R}{F}\right)^C$$

Our path is now clear. We merely need to divide both sides by whatever isn't n on the right hand side of the equation. Doing this, while also utilizing equation 4.6 to change the left hand side of the equation into a subtraction, we find:

Equation 9.21

$$\frac{\ln B - \ln\left(P - P\left(1 + \frac{R}{F}\right)^C + B\right)}{\ln\left(1 + \frac{R}{F}\right)^C} = n$$

Equation 9.21 above details how to find the number of payment periods n necessary to eliminate a dynamic compound interest loan provided we know B, P, C, F, and R. If this equation is true, and I see no holes in our derivation, then we can extrapolate this result to the necessary conditions for less simple and continuous compound interest. First setting C = F = 1 we find the less simple interest case.

$$\frac{\ln B - \ln(P - P(1 + R) + B)}{\ln(1 + R)} = n$$

Distributing the negative P through the parenthesis in the numerator and combining like terms produces:

Equation 9.22

$$\frac{\ln B - \ln(-PR + B)}{\ln(1 + R)} = n$$

Which gives us the simplified explicit solution for n during the less simple interest case. With this set of circumstances solved, let's now move on to the continuous compounding case correlating with setting C = F and then allowing F to approach infinity.

$$\frac{\ln B - \ln\left(P - P \lim_{F \to \infty}\left(1 + \frac{R}{F}\right)^F + B\right)}{\ln \lim_{F \to \infty}\left(1 + \frac{R}{F}\right)^F} = n$$

Now we simply substitute the equivalent statement with the Euler constant e, as assumed by equation 8.5, and we find:

$$\frac{\ln B - \ln(P - Pe^R + B)}{\ln e^R} = n$$

The denominator can be simplified further by using the algebraic properties of the logarithm, equation 4.3,

Equation 9.23

$$\frac{\ln B - \ln(P - Pe^R + B)}{R} = n$$

Equation 9.23 above is the simplified explicit solution to the number of payment period n provided we know B, R, and P.

Next we move to solving explicitly for P. Our starting point is the governing equation for dynamic compound interest with frequency at the time of complete payment.

$$0 = P\left(1 + \frac{R}{F}\right)^{nC} - B\left[\frac{1 - \left(1 + \frac{R}{F}\right)^{nC}}{1 - \left(1 + \frac{R}{F}\right)^{C}}\right]$$

Luckily for us, our equation only contains one P throughout the entire statement. Thus our first step is to separate the two addends which is accomplished by adding the bracketed term to both sides of the equation and then combining common terms.

$$B\left[\frac{1 - \left(1 + \frac{R}{F}\right)^{nC}}{1 - \left(1 + \frac{R}{F}\right)^{C}}\right] = P\left(1 + \frac{R}{F}\right)^{nC}$$

Now, simply divide both sides of the equation by whatever isn't P on the right hand side.

$$\frac{B}{\left(1 + \frac{R}{F}\right)^{nC}}\left[\frac{1 - \left(1 + \frac{R}{F}\right)^{nC}}{1 - \left(1 + \frac{R}{F}\right)^{C}}\right] = \frac{P\left(1 + \frac{R}{F}\right)^{nC}}{\left(1 + \frac{R}{F}\right)^{nC}}$$

Eliminate the common multiple on the right hand side produces our desired result:

Equation 9.24

$$\frac{B}{\left(1 + \frac{R}{F}\right)^{nC}}\left[\frac{1 - \left(1 + \frac{R}{F}\right)^{nC}}{1 - \left(1 + \frac{R}{F}\right)^{C}}\right] = P$$

And we have successfully solved the dynamic compound interest with frequency for P explicitly. Again we could easily extrapolate this result to the less simple and continuous compound interest by setting C = F = 1 and C = F approaching infinity respectively. First the less simple interest case:

$$\frac{B}{(1 + R)^n}\left[\frac{1 - (1 + R)^n}{1 - (1 + R)}\right] = P$$

And simplifying the bracketed denominator we find our less simple interest formula for P:

Equation 9.25

$$\frac{B}{(1 + R)^n}\left[\frac{1 - (1 + R)^n}{-R}\right] = P$$

Moving to the second set of conditions that coincide with continuously compounding interest:

$$\frac{B}{\lim\limits_{F\to\infty}\left(1+\frac{R}{F}\right)^{nF}}\left[\frac{1-\lim\limits_{F\to\infty}\left(1+\frac{R}{F}\right)^{nF}}{1-\lim\limits_{F\to\infty}\left(1+\frac{R}{F}\right)^{F}}\right]=P$$

Then utilizing the Euler constant form of the limit we find:

Equation 9.26

$$\frac{B}{e^{nR}}\left[\frac{1-e^{nR}}{1-e^{R}}\right]=P$$

After that monumental challenge of solving explicitly for n it was nice dealing with such a simple operation as solving explicitly for P.

Section 9.7 - Solving Explicitly for R, C, and F in Dynamic Compound Interest

Although difficult at some points, we eventually were able to power our way through the previous variables of the dynamic compound interest. But, for reasons that go beyond the scope of this text, we cannot solve explicitly for R, C, and F analytically, meaning through algebra alone. Mathematicians have found other ways around this problem by solving for R, C and F through numerical and/or graphical methods. One easy numerical method that I will suggest using is known as the interpolation method. To use the interpolation method for R you simply plug in the known values of P, n, B, C, and F and then just guess a value for R. With this hypothetical value in place of R we now have every bit of information needed to numerically combine the values together. This guess will of course nearly always be wrong, but how wrong it is, so to speak, gives us information that can be used to refine our guess. This information is determined by the result being larger or smaller than the desired numerical result. We then pick a refined hypothetical R, based upon the information gleaned beforehand, and plug this into the equation. Numerically solving the equation again will provide us more information that can be used to further refine our guess for R. Eventually, after repeating this process through several iterations, we will come to an exact or otherwise acceptable answer for R. This process can also be utilized for the variables C and F provided we know all other variable values. In fact, this process could even be used for any of the variables in any formula assuming we know all other bits of information.

Numerical examples of this process have been provided at the end of the chapter to help clarify and solidify your understanding.

It is important to note however, that we cannot use the results of this process to extrapolate to the less simple or continuously compounding interests. We will instead need to initiate the interpolation process with the proper governing equation. This means that if we desire to know the required R to make a dynamic continuously compounding statement valid, then we will need to begin with the governing equation for dynamic continuous compounding interest. Ditto for the less simple interest case.

Thus as we have just seen, algebra still has a few holes in it. At the present understanding of algebra it is impossible to solve explicitly for R. But perhaps with the knowledge you have accumulated through this text you will be inspired to look for new approaches to this problem and devise a way to actually solve this equation explicitly. The task will not be easy and some actually believe it to be impossible. But should you actually succeed in solving this vexing problem then you will have accomplished something that has never been done in the history of mankind. In fact there are many holes in mathematics that are actively being filled as we speak.

Perhaps even you will fill in and even add to the body of knowledge that is mathematics. The fact is that there is much work to be done and mathematicians can always use a helping hand. Best of Luck!

Section 9.8 – APR – Actual Annual Interest Rate

The amount of interest accumulated while compounding was shown to be effected by an increase of frequency. One should notice however that this increase occurred despite the fact that we never increased the actual interest rate R. Thus, as we well know by now, the simple interest rate r can be the same numerical value of the compound interest rate R, yet mean totally different amounts of actual interest accumulation. But how much more interest will the compounding create and could we find a simple interest rate that would effectively match the interest accumulated by a compound interest rate?

To clarify, consider we are quoted a compounded interest rate, continuous or otherwise, as x percent per year. What simple interest rate would be required to accumulate the exact same amount of interest over the course of a year?

To do this, we can utilize the concrete formulas that deal with these varying instances over the course of multiple time periods. First, let's recall the general formula for simple compound interest with frequency:

$$O_n = P\left(1 + \frac{R}{F}\right)^{nF}$$

And our general formula for simple interest was given as

$$o_n = p + npr$$

We will assume that both are in the same time period at the end of a year, meaning that n = n, and that the initial principals were equal. Our task then, is to find a corresponding simple interest rate that will cause the amount owed to be equal to the amount owed for the compounding interest rate case. Since the amount owed will be equal, by design, then we may state mathematically that

$$o_n = O_n$$

Which allows us to equate the two equivalent statements as well:

$$p + npr = P\left(1 + \frac{R}{F}\right)^{nF}$$

Before we get into the crux of the matter, let's simplify the equation so that we may make our life a little easier. First, recall that we assumed that the initial principal amounts were the same, in other words p = P

$$p + npr = p\left(1 + \frac{R}{F}\right)^{nF}$$

Dividing both sides by p will then eliminate all worry about the principal from our equation.

$$1 + nr = \left(1 + \frac{R}{F}\right)^{nF}$$

Let's assume that we knew R, the compound interest rate, and our goal was to solve the equation above explicitly for r, the simple interest rate. If we wanted to do this then we would need to isolate r on one side of the equation. This can be done by first subtracting one from both sides:

$$nr = \left(1 + \frac{R}{F}\right)^{nF} - 1$$

And then dividing both sides by n, the number of periods that have transpired

Equation 9.27

$$r = \frac{\left(1 + \frac{R}{F}\right)^{nF} - 1}{n}$$

Now if, and this is a big if, the interest rates are provided as an annual percentage, then we know for a fact that n dictates how many years have passed. Since this section is entitled actual annual interest rate, then we could argue that our goal corresponds with n equal to one, or one year of interest accumulation. This will simplify our equation to:

Equation 9.28

$$r = \left(1 + \frac{R}{F}\right)^{F} - 1$$

And we have solved explicitly for the actual annual simple interest rate for a corresponding annual compound interest rate. We can use this formula to find the equivalent simple interest rate, r, that will produce the same amount of debt in a year as a given compound interest rate R with a given frequency F, provided they are quoted as annual interest rates. If not, then we will need to utilize equation 9.27 to account for multiple periods of interest accumulation.

The important thing to note is that a single compound interest rate R does not directly correlate with a single simple interest rate r. The frequency F can and does affect the resulting simple interest rate r needed to produce the same amount of interest. Recall that as F became larger then the amount of interest accumulated also became larger which would necessarily require the resulting actual simple interest rate to become larger too.

So let's play a little game with the frequency and suppose that the frequency was equal to one, meaning that we have the least amount of frequency possible. Our equation would then reduce to:

$$r = (1 + R) - 1$$

Which, after being simplified by subtracting the common one's on the right hand side, shows that the compound annual interest rate R is exactly the same value as a purely simple annual interest rate. Furthermore, recall that a frequency equal to one was the same criteria needed for less simple interest. Thus less simple interest must match simple interest which directly reflects the assumptions we made when we approached less simple interest. It also tells us that punctual payment for a dynamic compound interest loan without frequency will match the simple interest rate, which again parallels our understanding of the effect frequency has on compound interest.

Choosing a frequency of one could be considered as the lower bound of interest accumulation for compound frequency. If we instead choose a larger value for F then this would serve to increase the accumulated interest for a single annual compound interest rate and therefore cause the corresponding actual annual simple interest rate to increase as well. This increase would continue until we reached the limiting maximum value of an infinite frequency. Thus our maximum actual annual simple interest rate for a corresponding annual compound interest rate R would be given as:

$$r = \lim_{F \to \infty} \left(1 + \frac{R}{F}\right)^F - 1$$

Which we could then replace the limit with the equivalent Euler constant form of the statement given by our assumed equation 8.5 to produce:

Equation 9.29

$$r = e^R - 1$$

Thus for any annual compound interest rate we can find the necessary annual simple interest rate that will produce the same amount of interest over the course of the year.

Section 9.9 – Total Cost of Loan:

The total cost of the loan is the amount needed to satisfy the entire outstanding principal and accumulated interest. If we can assume a constant payment each time period, then the total cost is a simple calculation.

Equation 9.30

$$TC = nb$$

Equation 9.30 above states that the Total Cost (TC) is equal to the number of payments needed to settle all debt multiplied by the amount paid each time period. Obviously knowledge of n and b is prerequisite information for this calculation. But given one, and the type of interest accumulation under scrutiny, then the other can be calculated with the tools developed in this chapter. One very important property of the total cost metric is the ability to directly compare the varying types of interest on an even footing. It can also serve as a gut check for a perspective borrower since it provides a firm written number representing the eventual price of whatever the borrower seeks to buy. I would recommend always performing the total cost calculation before signing any loan agreements to be sure the actual price isn't beyond your means or intentions.

Section 9.10 – Total Cost of Interest

The total cost of interest is a great eye opening tool for any potential borrower as it states exactly how much money you are paying to the lender beyond the value of the initial principal. The calculation can be made with knowledge of the original principal and the total cost of the loan.

Equation 9.31

$$TCI = TC - p$$

I would also recommend performing this calculation to get your head around the amount of money you're basically spending for the privilege of using someone else's money.

Section 9.11 – Numerical Examples:

Example 9.1 – Find the monthly payment necessary to pay off a loan of 150000 units of currency in 4 years under a 6 percent annual simple interest rate with monthly frequency.

- One will recall that the key to understanding simple interest loans is determining the critical time period which is given as the last time period to meet the qualifier

$$n < \frac{p}{b} + 1$$

- Unfortunately, as mentioned in the text, we need information on b to define the critical time period
- Hence we are in the classic catch 22, to find the value of b we need the value of b.
- One method is to assume that the ratio p/b is equal to an integer. If this is true, and the odds of it being true are quite slim, but if it is true then we could use the special case scenario to find b using equation 9.8

$$b = \frac{2p + pr + [(2p + pr)^2 + 8np^2r]^{\frac{1}{2}}}{4n}$$

- Of course we will need information on the values for the variables to proceed.
- The variable p is given directly in the example as 150000
- The variable r is quoted as a 6 percent annual rate with monthly frequency. To segment the annual rate into a monthly rate we must divide it by 12, and of course we will need to convert to decimal format to use it within the equation.

$$\frac{\frac{6}{12}}{100} = .005$$

- One should recall also that the reference time period for a particular problem is determined by the payment period, however we don't even have a payment let alone a payment period. So let's just assume one, let's call it monthly seeing as we already went through all that trouble finding the monthly interest rate. Thus we will need to get the number of passed time periods into a month as well. 4 multiplied by 12 is 48 months. So n is equal to 48.
- With all of the needed variable defined we can calculate to find:

$$b = 3470.48$$

- As can clearly be seen, p/b does not equal a whole number and thus fails our test to be included in the special case scenario. But fear not, because this result is in fact close enough to the actual answer that we can use it to calculate the critical time period.

$$\frac{p}{b} + 1 = 44.221 \dots$$

- Thus the critical time period for this example is the last integer to be less than 44.221…, which is 44. With this information in tow, we can use equation 9.16 to give a precise solution for the necessary payment size to satisfy the loan

$$b = \frac{2p + 2prn_c}{2n + rn_c(n_c - 1)}$$

- After calculating we find:

$$b = 3470.51$$

- And the precise answer has been shown to be only 3 cents larger than the approximate answer.
- With such a small discrepancy between the actual and approximate value, one may wonder why we even care to calculate the actual answer. The short answer is because this is mathematics and we must try to be as precise as we can be. But in all honesty, if you want to simply use the special case scenario for a rough answer to the simple interest payment then be my guest.

Example 9.2 – What is the largest loan you could take out on a continuously compounding interest rate with monthly frequency of 6 percent annual for 20 years with a maximum monthly payment of 2000 units of currency?

- Since this example uses a monthly payment cycle, we will define the time period reference as a month. Thus we will need to get all of the variables in terms of their monthly value
- 20 years times 12 months a year gives a current time period of n equal to 240
- 6 percent annual interest will need to be divided by 100 to convert to the decimal format, and then be divided by 12 to achieve the monthly decimal value. Thus R equals .005
- The continuously compounding interest was solved explicitly for P in equation 9.26 as

$$\frac{B}{e^{nR}}\left[\frac{1 - e^{nR}}{1 - e^{R}}\right] = P$$

- Plugging in the known variables values we find an initial principal amount of

$$P = 278824.09$$

- This result means that if a 2000 unit monthly payment were possible then a loan of 278824.09 could be covered by the end of 20 years

Example 9.3 – Determine the total cost of the previous loan and the amount paid in interest to the lender.

- To compute the total cost of loan we would need to use equation 9.30, which is the amount you pay per time period multiplied by the number of time periods.
- The time period from the last example was 240, while the payment was 2000.

$$TC = nB = 480000$$

- 480000 units of currency to ultimately cover a mere 278824.09 in initial principal. Since we know both the total coast and the initial principal, then we can compute the total interest paid using equation 9.31

$$TCI = TC - P = 201175.90$$

- Which is 72 percent of the original money borrowed

Example 9.4 – Determine the number of payments necessary to satisfy 250,000 units of currency compound interest loan with a .005 monthly decimal interest rate at a monthly payment of 2000 and 2250. Then determine the total cost of the loan for each payment amount.

- Since the payment and interest accumulation occur simultaneously on a monthly time scale, we can use equation 9.22 to determine the number of months necessary to satisfy the loan.

$$\frac{\ln B - \ln(-PR + B)}{\ln(1 + R)} = n$$

- First we will let B equal 2000, P equal 250000, and R equal .005 to compute a total number of passed periods of:

$$n = 196.655 \dots$$

- The total cost of this loan can be found by multiplying the number of periods and the period payment.

$$TC = 393311.72$$

- Next we will let b equal 2500 to satisfy the second part of the example. Doing this we can calculate the number of passed time periods as

$$n = 162.591 \dots$$

- The total cost is found by equation 9.30

$$TC = 365830.14$$

- This means that attaching a 250 unit additional payment to the monthly bill can save a total of 27481.58 units of currency for the lender on the total repayment of the loan. Not too shabby.